# Making It in Commodities

*by Mark Weinberg*

Bonus Books, Chicago

90  89  88  87  86                    5  4  3  2  1

Library of Congress Catalog Card Number: 85-73452

International Standard Book Number: 0-933893-06-X

**Bonus Books, Inc.**
160 East Illinois Street
Chicago, Illinois 60611

Printed in the United States of America

*For my mom,*
*Elaine Weinberg,*
*with love*

# Contents

# Acknowledgments

Thanks to my brother, Lee, who let me use—well, steal—his computer to write this book. I hope I'm half as good a brother to him as he is to me. I love him. Thanks, too, to the people at the Chicago Board of Trade and other exchanges who shared their knowledge with me: Dan Clifford, Mitchell Cohodes, Brian Durkin, Todd Feldman, Tom Fitzgerald, Avis Frommer, Rick Hildebrand, McCabe Hurley, Gary Gibson, Cary Goodman, Joel Kanter, Dave Kavanagh, Barry Levin, Ronald Manaster, Janice Mentzer, Gordy Schwabe, Tom Schwarz, Tim Sheehan, Kathy Siedleki, Jeff Soman, and Bob Welch.

# 1

## What's This Book About?

A lot of books promise to make their readers rich trading commodities. Most have catchy titles like *How to Turn Your Spare $5,000 into $500,000 in Your Free Time Through Commodities Trading* or *How to Make a Million: A Commodity System for Winners*. These books offer anyone with $9.95 a chance to make a fortune. I would like to write a book called *How I Made $38 Million in Only Six Months Trading Commodities*. But get-rich-quick books are like instant weight-reduction pills and miraculous hair tonics. The only people these books help are their authors and publishers. I'm skeptical that anybody who could turn $5,000 into $500,000 would sell that knowledge for only $9.95. At best, these books offer readers some of the basic, time-tested guidelines to intelligent speculation. At worst, they are filled with bad advice about speculating and inaccuracies about the market.

Not everyone gets rich from trading commodities. These

books rarely mention that over 80 percent of the people who speculate lose. The speculators who do win probably are not the ones who learned from a book. The small speculator competes against some of the world's largest banks, trading companies, and professional traders. And worse, a small speculator must pay larger commission rates and usually gives up what is known as the trading edge—the ability to get the best possible trading price at the time of the trade's execution. If you asked 100 floor traders on any exchange if small outside customers should speculate, the answer would be a unanimous "No way." A small percentage of outside speculators do succeed in the market through luck or superior knowledge. But here's rule number one: if you have to buy a book to learn how to speculate, you shouldn't be doing it.

There is, however, one time-tested path to success in commodities: ignore the get-rich-quick temptations and make it your career. The best advice for doing well requires only three short words: Get a job.

This book doesn't pretend to teach the secrets of successful trading. No book can teach that. Trading is a skill best learned by experience and observation. Instead, this book provides the information necessary to get a job on an exchange floor. It offers sound and practical advice about the commodities industry, details the various entry-level positions on an exchange floor, and offers information on obtaining a membership, even with limited funds. It features the stories of several young men and women currently working on the floor of the Chicago Board of Trade (CBOT), the Chicago Mercantile Exchange (CME), and the Commodity Exchange (COMEX) in New York City.

They provide revealing and invaluable information about the frustrations and joys, the ins-and-outs, and the ups-and-downs of beginning a career in commodities. The book isn't meant to be a primer on commodities. I don't dwell on the technical aspects of the marketplace, but when you read the book, you can't help but learn a lot about how the futures markets operate. But the floor is where you'll learn the lessons you won't forget.*

So what good is a commodities book that doesn't promise to make you rich or even to explain the difference between a tandem and a butterfly spread? This is an honest book. I don't promise to make you a millionaire, but I want to point you in the direction that can take you there. I think this book is one of the few books that can legitimately call itself a get-rich-quick plan for a profession in which thousands of career opportunities exist and remarkable financial rewards are possible. Every successful young trader and broker is walking proof of this.

### Who Should Read This Book?

This book isn't for everybody who wants to be a floor trader. Why? Because it's easy to *become* a trader. All it takes is enough money and a relatively clean criminal record. You can buy a membership tommorrow and begin trading in weeks. If you think you know it all and want to jump into the trading pits without any experience on the trading floor, you don't need this book. Of course, the odds are good that you will be broke within a year—sadder, as they say, and wiser—but you can try.

This book is written specifically for those who want to learn the business the right way—from the bottom up. It's no secret in the commodities industry and it's a fundamental assumption of this book that the best and most successful floor traders and brokers are generally the ones who have worked themselves up the hierarchy on the trading floor.

---

*For an excellent introduction to those aspects of the futures market, I recommend that you read *Commodities Trading Manual,* a 286-page manual published by the CBOT. It covers all the technical aspects of futures trading.

But success doesn't come easily. Some people say that one out of seven traders are successful—others say one out of ten. No one knows for sure. They don't keep box scores on the failures. But any way you look at it, the odds are against anybody's becoming a successful trader or broker. But the odds improve tremendously when you play the game a certain way. There's no precise path that every successful trader has taken, but this book describes the most common ones.

Some started broke with little or no education. Some started with a good education and the support of a wealthy family behind them. But most successful traders have one thing in common: they began slowly, learning the business step by step. This book describes those steps.

### Do You Need a Relative in the Business to Get a Job?

No. That's one of the many myths about the industry. Do connections help? Of course. Are there a lot of relatives who trade on the exchange floors? Yes. Does that mean that the exchange is some kind of exclusive club? Not at all.

Is it a matter of keeping it all in the family? I don't think so. People who are exposed to the industry tend to be attracted to it. If you haven't grown up with the business, it's not a career that a youngster learns about in school. You don't hear too many kids in the playground say, "I want to be a scalper when I grow up."

Prior to the early 70s, the industry was something few people knew about, even in Chicago. One trader told me that even though he grew up in Chicago, he didn't know the CBOT existed until after he graduated from college. Since then, the industry has boomed and it's no longer a well-kept secret. Young people flock to the exchanges—some with family connections, but most without. Of the ten people I interviewed in chapter 3, three had family connections and seven didn't. In the older exchanges such as the CBOT and the CME, there is a tradition. It is not uncommon to find several generations of traders who are relatives. This is not the case in the newer exchanges such as the Chicago Board of Options Exchange (CBOE) and the New York Futures Exchange (NYFE), which are too young to have that tradition.

It would be dishonest to downplay the importance of connections. "Success" books talk about "hard work and determination" and "positive mental attitude" as the secrets to success, but a career book should be more honest: connections help in every phase of the game. They help, first, by allowing you to get a foot in the door and, second, by having people take an interest in you, teach you, and, if need be, protect you.

But many successful traders didn't have family down on the floor. Anybody with a little persistence can get a foot in the door. Sure, Daddy might have to make only one phone call to get Sonny a job as a runner, but you'll get in, even without connections, if you pound on a few doors. Once you get the job, it helps to have someone looking out for you when you step into the trading pit, but even if you don't, you'll make connections once you're working. Indeed, the purpose of this book is to put you in a good position to make connections. One of the benefits of working as a runner, phone clerk, or trade checker is that you will meet people and make friends. If you don't have the money to buy a membership, you'll have to befriend someone who does. That's why people work as brokers' and traders' assistants. But more on that later.

### What Kind of Education Do I Need?

Success is open to all. The markets don't discriminate. Ivy-league graduate or high-school drop-out—the market is brutally objective and rewards only one's trading skill.

Unlike the legal, medical, and banking professions, commodities trading does not reward academic credentials. Two to four years of post-graduate work and as much as $50,000 in tuition are required before someone can enter those professions. In futures trading formal education is irrelevant to success. Some old-time traders say that a first-rate education can hinder trading success. Their logic is that too much analysis can stifle a trader's instincts. Traders make hundreds of split-second decisions every day and they can't afford to analyze too critically the merits of every single trade. Rumor has it that at least one East Coast commodity trading company refuses to hire anybody with more than an undergraduate education. Their rationale is that too much education eats away at the raw instincts that a successful trader must have.

Of course, many successful traders have received excellent educations, but most of the top floor traders and brokers have received their educations on the streets. Harvard, Yale, and Stanford have traditionally been the favorite breeding grounds of corporate lawyers and investment bankers, but the trading pit is unimpressed by academic degrees. It doesn't ask to look at your diploma before it takes away your money. One successful broker in the Board of Trade bond pit, who has an MBA from the University of Chicago, told a *Washington Monthly* reporter a couple of years ago, "I had all these academic credentials and when I got down here I was told I knew too much. One guy took me aside and said, 'See that guy over there? He used to be a furniture saleman. He's going to do a lot better than you are.' And you know what? He did."

As the industry continues to grow in both volume and importance in the world economy, a larger number of business school graduates will be attracted to the markets, but in the trading pits their credentials will still be worthless. One trader with a PhD in economics told me, "Around here, PhD means one thing: Piled Higher and Deeper."

### Do I Have the Right Type of Personality for a Trader?

Some books on commodities suggest that good traders all share common personality traits and that it's possible to tell who will and won't succeed as a trader. Baloney. In his book,

*The Traders,* Sonny Kleinfield gives a description of traders so general that it's virtually meaningless. It could apply to almost anyone:

> There is a class of people who don't like to take orders. They don't like sitting at desks and answering incessantly trilling phones. Back-patting and other distasteful rituals of office politics are not for them. They have an exceedingly high opinion of themselves and they like to dream big dreams.

Some books and articles like to portray the commodities trader as a twentieth-century cowboy. It makes great copy and sells magazines to show the trading pit as the last outpost of unfettered capitalism, where machismo, vigor, and bold adventurism reign supreme. It sounds romantic, but most of these descriptions are exaggerated, if not downright inaccurate. A typical paragraph from one of these descriptions might read:

> The risks and fast-paced action of the commodities pits exclude everybody but the most individualistic and risk-loving types. It's a business that demands steel nerves and iron discipline. Traders live and thrive on a roller-coaster ride of economic uncertainty. Ultimately, even the strongest among them succumbs to the emotional stress.

Other books portray the typical trader as a money-hungry, free-wheeling rake. In his book *The New Gatsbys,* Bob Tamarkin paints with a broad stroke:

> They are the ultimate consumers, graduates cum laude of economist Stanley Jevon's so-called hedonist school. . . . Money, not power, is their ultimate aphrodisiac. . . . They consume like people who regret the missed opportunities of life and then by some magic are given another chance.

But each of these descriptions shows only one side of the coin. They play up the young hot-shots who drive Mercedes, snort cocaine, and buy condominiums for their mistresses.

What they omit to mention is that some of the best traders are cautious and prudent and capitalize on their ability to minimize risks. The point is that the personalities of traders are as varied as the personalities of lawyers, doctors, and plumbers.

Most traders enjoy working independently, possess a strong entrepeneurial bent, and have a desire to make a lot of money, but then so do most people. Practically the only common trait among them is the willingness to put up with the loud noise on the trading floor. Sometimes, the free-wheeling gambler profits hugely as a trader, but some of the most successful traders better fit the image of a conservative, risk-averse banker.

You can't limit successful floor trading to one personality type, and nobody can tell before the fact who will succeed and who will fail in the trading pits. In fact, it's probably closer to the truth to believe that a person of any personality type can be a successful trader. As one successful soybean trader at the CBOT told me, "If you can put your pants on, you can learn how to trade."

### What's So Special About Commodities?

When the famous bank robber Willy Sutton was asked why he robbed banks, he said, "Because that's where they keep the money." Sutton's straightforward response applies equally well to commodities. Few other professions offer the chance to make so much money so fast. Twenty-six-year-olds can make enough money to retire. Old pros have made enough money to buy major sports franchises. Commodities trading is a game in which even when you're good, you're great. There are no statistics on what the average trader and broker earn, but good traders—average traders—commonly earn annual incomes over $100,000, while the top traders and brokers can earn over $1 million a year. The signs of success can be seen almost everywhere:

• In the articles in popular magazines, which feature the latest street-smart kid who quit a good job and turned $20,000 into $20 million;

• In the barroom gossip, where you hear about a guy's best friend who in 1976 quit his job in a gas station to take a job as a $60-a-week runner and now earns close to $5,000 a day as a floor broker;

• In the skyline of Chicago, where the world's two largest commodity exchanges, the CBOT and the CME, recently completed construction of new exchange buildings, costing $103 million and $57 million, respectively;

• In the vanity license plates on the Mercedes or Rolls Royce of traders which, advertising the source of their owners' wealth, read "HOGS," "BELLIES," "BULL," "BEAR," "CBOT 1," and even, believe it or not, "GREED."

But commodities trading isn't a guaranteed path to riches. I don't want to encourage the myth that all traders are rolling in cash. Most traders' salaries do not approach the salaries of most top bankers, lawyers, or doctors. It's generally accepted that 80 percent of the money is made by 20 percent of the traders. The majority of traders are competing for a relatively small piece of the pie.

### Is Now a Good Time to Enter the Industry?

If history is any guide, yes. The last decade has been the most active and innovative time in futures history. In contract volume, number of participants, innovative contracts, and dollar value, the late 1970s and early 1980s have seen an explosion in the industry. Commodities trading has always been one of the fastest games in town, but now it's also one of the fastest-growing games in town. The career opportunities and potential profits have never been greater either.

### How Fast Has the Industry Grown?

By leaps and bounds. The annual volume information of the Futures Industry Association shows that from 1970 to 1984 trading multiplied an unbelievable 11 times, increasing from 13.6 million contracts to over 149 million. In 1985 this trend continued.

### What's the Reason for the Recent Surge?

One of the biggest reasons for the sky-rocketing growth of the industry has been the introduction of financial futures. Since the opening in 1972 of currency futures on the International Monetary Exchange of the CME and the subsequent introduction at the CBOT of GNMA mortgage-backed certificates, the first interest rate futures contract, financial futures have accounted for an increasingly larger percentage of total futures trading. The most successful futures contract in the world now is the treasury bond futures contract at the CBOT.

### What Other Contracts Have Helped Spur the Industry?

The most exciting and promising new contracts since the introduction of interest rate futures are stock index futures and options on futures. Introduced in 1982, both of these new concepts in futures trading have caught on rapidly and played an important part in the volume surge over the past three years. The Kansas City Board of Trade introduced the first stock index futures contract in January 1982, based on the Value Line Index, which traded a respectable 528,743 contracts in its first year. But the trend-setting Kansas City contract has not been able to capture the bulk of market volume.

In 1982, three different exchanges began trading options on futures. The CBOT introduced options on treasury bond futures; the COMEX in New York, gold options; and the Cocoa Exchange in New York, sugar options. Options on futures have increased as rapidly in volume as stock index futures.

### The Exchanges: Where and What?

Ten exchanges are active in the United States today. Well, that's not entirely accurate—a few exchanges, such as the Chicago Rice & Cotton Exchange, which traded a total of 2,978 contracts in 1984, are so small that I'm not going to list them here. The ten major exchanges are these:

### Chicago

Chicago Board of Trade (CBOT)
141 W. Jackson
Chicago, IL 60604
Tel: 312-435-3500

Chicago Mercantile Exchange (CME)
30 S. Wacker
Chicago, IL 60606
Tel: 312-930-1000

Mid-American Commodity Exchange (MIDAM)
444 W. Jackson
Chicago, IL 60606
Tel: 312-341-3000

### Kansas City

Kansas City Board of Trade (KCBOT)
4800 Main Street
Kansas City, MO 64112
Tel: 816-753-7500

## Minneapolis

Minneapolis Grain Exchange (MGE)
150 Grain Exchange Building
Minneapolis, MN 55415
Tel: 612-338-6212

## New York

New York Cotton & Citrus Exchange (NYCE)
Commodity Exchange Center
4 World Trade Center
New York, NY 10048
Tel: 212-938-2650

Commodity Exchange, Inc. (COMEX)
Commodity Exchange Center
4 World Trade Center
New York, NY 10048
Tel: 212-938-2900

New York Coffee, Sugar and
Cocoa Exchange, Inc (CSC)
Commodity Exchange Center
4 World Trade Center
New York, NY 10048
Tel: 212-938-2800

New York Futures Exchange (NYFE)
20 Broad Street
New York, NY 10005
Tel: 212-623-4949

New York Mercantile Exchange (NYME)
Commodity Exchange Center
4 World Trade Center
New York, NY 10048
Tel: 212-938-2222

## What Are the Fastest-Growing Exchanges?

Not all exchanges show the same growth. In 1984 the fastest-growing exchange was the NYME (see Appendix 2 for details). Volume increased 36 percent in the year, practically doubling the next closest rivals, the two industry giants, the CBOT and the CME, whose volume increased 15 percent and 17 percent respectively. The only other exchange to post an increase in 1984 was the KCBOT, increasing 12 percent. And over the past five years, the fastest-growing exchange by far was the NYFE, which increased 1,913 percent, over five times more than any other exchange. In the same period, the NYME saw a 363 percent increase, while the CME increased 100 percent. In comparison, the largest exchange, the CBOT, increased a relatively modest 64 percent.

But these numbers are somewhat deceptive. It's obviously easier for a smaller exchange to increase its percentage of growth than for a larger exchange. A more revealing number than simple volume increase is an exchange's share of total market volume. When this measure is used, the two largest exchanges, the CBOT and the CME, reveal their dominance of the industry. Between 1983 and 1984, both exchanges increased their market share of volume: the CBOT from 45 percent to almost 47 percent and the CME from 27 percent to 28 percent, increasing their combined market share from 72 percent to 75 percent.

## Where to Start: New York, Chicago, Kansas City, or Minneapolis?

I don't want to recommend one exchange or one city over another, and yet it's difficult for me not to emphasize Chicago.

Chicago is the center of the industry. The CBOT and CME are the industry's two volume leaders, but their prominence goes beyond the statistics. Why? Because there is some irony to the success of futures exchanges. As we have indicated, the larger exchanges have enjoyed the most success in recent years from the introduction of interest-rate futures, options on futures, and stock-index futures. This confirms the well-accepted maxim of futures trading that the markets must have local support to succeed. Although the potential number of hedgers for a particular commodity may have no limit, no market will succeed without the support of speculative local traders. Speculators, however, will only supply liquidity to markets in which price movements are fast, execution of trades reliable, and trading potentially profitable— translated, they prefer the established exchanges with good track records. The well-established exchanges then attract the hedgers and, in the end, prosper when smaller exchanges don't. When you start out, of course, geography is an important factor: it may make sense for you to start out in the exchange nearest your home, especially at a runner's salary.

I don't mean to dwell on Chicago or slight any of the other exchanges. New York, Kansas City, and Minneapolis offer great opportunities. But the choice between trading at a big exchange and trading at a small exchange isn't the same as deciding whether to work for a big company or a small one. In the business world, a smaller company may offer advantages that a larger company doesn't, including opportunities for growth, flexibility, and power. But in commodities, a less active exchange means primarily one thing: less chance to profit. The larger exchanges also, somewhat paradoxically, lead the industry in innovation.

In describing floor operations, I focus on Chicago. Slight variations in these procedures occur at other exchanges in other cities. At the COMEX, in New York, for instance, trades are checked throughout the day, whereas in Chicago the majority of trades are checked after the market's close. But the basic operations are the same everywhere. I use Chicago as the standard because I know it best.

### Will the Rapid Growth Continue?

Nobody knows the answer. A trader judging the situation might go with the trend and say the growth probably will continue. (One of the first trading rules everyone learns is "The trend is your friend.") Good reasons for optimism abound. Most industry observers are bubbling with optimism over future prospects.

Experts believe that financial futures have thus far given only a slight indication of their potential growth. Estimates vary concerning what percentage of large-money managers—those with pension funds, insurance companies, and savings and loans—currently use financial futures as a hedging device or as part of a diversified portfolio. But by almost everyone's account, the number is small compared to what it will be in coming years.*

A small percentage of money managers currently use the markets. For example, in a 1984 survey** of 648 investment management firms, only sixty-nine of them reported using fixed income futures and only forty-six reported using stock index futures, 11 percent and 7 percent respectively. In a 1985 survey of the top 200 pension funds, only forty used financial futures, an increase from thirteen in 1982 and twenty-six in 1984. These numbers still fall significantly below future projections. Don't forget: financial futures are a baby in the investment community. Most money managers have yet to warm up to them. Interest rate futures are only a decade old, and stock index futures and options are less

---

*See chapter 4 (pp. 127-129) for an analysis of the likely consequences of increased participation by large money managers
**Pension Asset Growth Stunted in 1984," *Pension & Investment Age,* Jan. 21, 1985, Vol. 13, No. 2.

than five years old. As time passes and managers become more familiar with these instruments, the markets surely will benefit.

Another piece of good news for futures is the conservative economic trend in this country, particularly the increasing faith in market forces. In the past, regulatory measures have limited the use of financial futures by depository institutions and money managers. Initially, the government was skeptical of financial futures and it placed harsh restrictions on the use of futures by banks, savings and loans, and large-money managers. But the restrictions have been eased as people realize that financial futures can be used as tools to avoid unnecessary risk. They provide corporations, banks, debt instrument dealers, and institutional investors with the ability to hedge against adverse market movements.*

### Isn't There Any Bad News About the Future?

Not all the statistical information is rosy. Although 1984 saw a 6.8 percent increase in total futures trading (not including options on futures), seven out of the eleven exchanges had lower volume than in 1983. At the country's largest exchange, the CBOT, which saw a 15 percent increase in volume in 1984, nine out of thirteen contracts had lower volume. Similarly, at the CME, fourteen out of nineteen contracts, including the currencies, had lower volume.

One of the biggest worries of exchange officials is that the recent influx of new contracts has spread the industry too thin. The surge in volume has been accompanied by heated competition among exchanges to introduce new contracts at a fast pace.

---

*If you're interested in a complete overview of the evolution of the regulatory laws governing national banks, state banks, insurance companies and pension funds, see the *Handbook of Financial Futures* (Chapter 20). But I am writing to help you get your first job, and I've already told you what you need to know about regulation to do that.

A large number of new proposals is a sign of a strong and prosperous industry. But many industry officials are afraid that an excessive number of contracts will, in the long run, harm liquidity. They charge that the pool of new futures and options contracts is running ahead of investor awareness and market need. No one is certain of the demoralizing effect an unsuccessful contract has on the industry, but many officials fear that too many failures will eventually begin to sap public confidence in the industry.

Another serious doubt is that the great surge of the 70s and 80s was the temporary result of a shaky world economy and that greater economic stability will be bad news for futures. History shows that the futures industry as a whole thrives in unstable economic periods. Bad times are good for futures: Inflation means uncertainty, which means price fluctuations, which means trading activity, which means busy markets, which, they hope, means profits for the pit traders. The one sure way to kill interest rate futures is not through government regulation but through stable interest rates.

### And the Verdict Is?

Neither the good news nor the bad offers any definite clues about the future of futures. I tend to be bullish on the future. But perhaps the last word should go to a retired soybean trader who told me that people have been writing off the industry as long as he can remember. "After the second world war, people said the industry was through. And almost every ten years the same thing is said. But it keeps on growing anyway," he said. "I don't know why things should be different now."

# 2

## The Why's, What's, and How's of Floor Jobs

It's ironic, but even with computerized technology and elaborate systems developed to beat the markets, actual floor operations can be described in one paragraph:

> Phone clerks answer the trilling phones that circle the trading pits. They write down customer orders, time stamp the orders, and hand them to runners, who carry the orders to the brokers. A broker either fills an order immediately or puts it in the deck, depending on the order price. Each fill is immediately reported to the quotations clerks, who watch the pit from a booth to the side of the pit and electronically relay the changing prices to the computerized boards that cover the exchange walls and to the tickertapes over the world. Runners pick up the filled orders and bring them to the phone clerks, who time stamp them and call customers to report the fills.

If you understand that, you're ahead of most young people who go down to the exchanges. If you don't, don't panic. I

promise that no one—no employer, no firm, no trader—
expects you to know anything about the industry before you
start. As one clerk told me, "No one knows anything when
they start. It's like going to school when you come down here.
There's nothing you can do beforehand to prepare for it."
The only people who are in for big trouble are the ones who
come down thinking they know what's going on.

I can't show you one simple path to a successful career. I
can offer practical advice about starting in the industry. It's
a route that most successful traders and brokers have followed and that you should know.

### Should I Get a Job on the Trading Floor?

Definitely. If your goal is to be a broker or independent
trader, the best jobs for any newcomer are those on the floor.
Why? Because there's no better place to learn trading skills
than on the trading floor (other than in the trading pit itself,
but there the cost of each lesson is prohibitively expensive
and people lose their houses trying to learn). Trading is a skill
best learned through observation and experience rather
than instruction. It is a skill that can be learned but not
taught.

Even the lowest-paying floor job offers a person the chance
to see top traders in action, to recognize various market patterns, and to develop a sense of market movement. Yogi
Berra's baseball advice also is appropriate for the floor: "You
can observe a lot by watching."

Working on the floor also gives a person an opportunity
to make connections. I don't mean dishonest connections.
I mean making the most of an opportunity to forge friend-
ships, impress people with your competence, and ultimately
earn their trust. That's how you move on to better, higher-
paying jobs. The commodities industry is based on trust—
billions of dollars worth of transactions occur daily based on

a flick of the wrist or a shake of the head. Connections are doubly important for the young person who doesn't have the money to buy a membership and must earn a trader's or broker's trust to get into the pits. Opportunity doesn't knock every day, but recently in the commodities industry it's been knocking a lot. If you're on your toes, you won't miss a chance.

### Is Age an Important Factor?

Yes. The younger you begin your career, the better. Why? Because the younger you are the more chance you have to observe the market and learn the skills and discipline necessary to be a successful trader without feeling the pressure of having to make a large income. Recently, it's been quite common for lawyers, police officers, professors, and other professionals to change careers in midstream to become commodity traders. These people are likely to feel pressure to earn a big income, yet often they can't afford the time to learn the business from the bottom up. Instead, they jump into the trading pits without any experience and usually lose money.

"The two years I worked as a broker's assistant were the lousiest two years of my life," a treasury bond broker now earning as much as $400,000 a year at the Chicago Board of Trade (CBOT) told me. "At thirty, I quit my job as a medical supplies salesman to work at the Board. I earned barely $200 a week for two years—and had to support my wife and two kids on it. Fortunately, things worked out for me, but not everybody is so lucky." The pressure is even greater for an independent trader who, coming to the markets relatively late in life, must learn the business and support a family at the same time. The result: every dollar counts, there's no room for error, and each trade becomes an extra-pressure situation.

### What Are the Best Floor Jobs?

There are three different routes to working on the trading floor. Each will be described in depth.

1. *Brokerage House*

The easiest and most common way of getting a job on the floor is with a brokerage house. Even in tight job markets, jobs usually can be found with one of the many member brokerage houses on an exchange floor. At a brokerage firm you can learn all the various sides of a commodity career. In just one year, a person might work in several different jobs, moving from runner to phone clerk to trade checker. Each of these jobs will be described in detail later in this chapter.

2. *Broker's and Trader's Assistant*

This is another good way to enter the business, but these jobs are hard to get. Usually you have to know someone well or already have proved yourself in some other job on the floor before a broker or trader will hire you. The biggest benefit of working as an assistant is that you will be working for a person or persons who may take a lasting interest in your future. Recently, given the huge increases in trading volume and the explosion of new contracts, working as a broker's assistant has been particularly rewarding. Many broker's assistants have quickly found themselves brokers when the broker's own business grew too large to handle alone.

3. *The Commodity Exchange*

A less desirable but still rewarding path to the trading floor is working for the exchange itself. It is a less direct route to the floor than the others, but the larger exchanges offer a number of good jobs for the newcomer. The smaller exchanges, whose staffs are proportionally smaller, do not offer the opportunities that the larger exchanges do. Nevertheless, several successful Chicago commodity traders began working for one of the local exchanges.

### What Is a Brokerage House?

Brokerage houses are firms that transact commodity business on the exchange floor on behalf of customers, who may be either commercial users of the commodity markets or private investors. They are the link between the exchange and customers. For a commission fee, brokerage houses offer fast and easy access to the exchange floor. They eliminate the need for individuals to be present at the exchange to make a trade.

In addition, they accept the financial obligations of their customers' trades and, thus, eliminate the risk of individual customers defaulting on their trades. Of course, customers are expected to pay their debts, and firms require them to carry a specific amount of good-faith money, called margin, to cover the risks inherent in any trade. But as far as the exchange is concerned, a brokerage firm is ultimately responsible for its customers' trades. The brokerage house is responsible for debts that its customers can't pay. Brokerage houses keep the names of their clients in strict confidence. All trades are made in the name of the brokerage house.

A typical exchange floor has three types of brokerage houses: retail, commercial, and small professional houses. All three perform the same basic function of buying and selling contracts for the customer and accepting financial responsibility for the customer's trades. However, each appeals to a different sector of the market. It's difficult to pigeonhole most firms as one type or another. Most are a hybrid of two or three types.

A. *Retail firms* include the huge, full-service, national brokerage houses like Merrill Lynch and Smith-Barney. These firms are members of most, if not all, of the world's stock and commodity exchanges. Their customers include large corporations and small investors. Generally, these houses charge the highest commission rates of the three types because of their full-service commitment. Their large research departments provide extensive information to their clients. In addition, each client has an account executive who should be knowledgeable about the markets and who can give timely buy and sell signals to clients.

B. *Commercial firms* can be broken down into two groups: (1) private trading companies and (2) firms specializing in institutional accounts. Private trading companies trade exclusively for their own accounts. They may trade only one commodity or they may trade many different commodities. They may vary in size from a simple, two-person operation, to a huge company like Salomon Brothers. Firms specializing in institutional accounts deal almost exclusively with commercial hedgers, including banks, savings and loans, large money managers, and government security dealers. These firms provide their clients with superior service by having account executives on the trading floor who are prepared to give up-to-the-second market analysis to the institutional clients.

C. *Professional trading companies* focus on the local pit traders and small professional traders. Since these firms do not offer full service to their clients, they are able to charge lower commission rates. They expect their clients to make their own investment decisions. They do not have account executives holding the clients' hand every step of the way. They offer direct access to the trading floor and quick execution of trades, but none of the frills of a retail firm.

### Which Type of Brokerage House Offers the Best Jobs?

Even though there are three types of brokerage firms, the process of filling an order on the floor is the same for every type of firm. However, I don't mean it doesn't matter where you work.

Common sense says that there are important differences between large and small firms. A large, national, retail brokerage house like Merrill Lynch offers workers incomparable amounts of market information and analysis, as well as state-of-the art equipment. But, of course, an individual on the floor of an exchange risks being lost in the shuffle of a huge firm. A smaller local firm, on the other hand, will give you more personal attention and there's a better chance that someone will recognize your ability and help you move up in the hierarchy.

My experience is typical. I worked for a small, professional brokerage house at the CBOT. In only four months of employment, I worked as a runner, phone clerk, and trade checker, after which I began trading for myself. I was in a particular hurry to begin trading, and if you are also, a small firm probably will give you the chance to do more in a relatively short time than a larger firm will.

### What Jobs Will You Find at Brokerage Firms?

Every firm offers five basic floor jobs, all of which are excellent preparation for a career as an independent trader or broker:

1. Runner
2. Phone Clerk
3. Trade Checker
4. Floor Manager
5. Margin Clerk

### RUNNER
Hours: Market
Average Salary: $10,000-$15,000

Working as a runner is the easiest and fastest way to get yourself on the floor. It's proven to be one one of the best first-steps for beginning a career in commodities. Ask five traders how they started in the business and three probably will say as a runner. A runner is the twentieth century's version of indentured servitude. Ask a broker what a runner does, and he'll say, "He's the punk who brings me the orders." Ask a trader what a runner does, and he'll say, "He's the peon who goes downstairs to get my Sox tickets." It's not a job for those who think they're above doing petty errands. The position is low paying and the hours are short, but the future is loaded with possibilities, which makes up for a lot of the headaches of the job.

### What Are a Runner's Responsibilities?

**Customer Orders:** The basic responsibility of a runner is to carry customer orders to and from the order desk and the broker in the pit. Runners must carry the orders as quickly as possible (but always without running, which is forbidden at all major exchanges). Good runners always read the order carefully to note how close the order price is to the current market price to gauge the urgency of handing the order to the broker.

**Spread Prices:** It's also the runner's job to keep track of changing spread prices so that the phone clerks can report the latest prices to the clients. A spread price is the difference in price between two or more different commodities. Unlike single commodity prices which can be found through a quick glance in the pit or easily read off the huge quotations boards, spread quotes must be updated regularly with the brokers.

**Time and Sales:** In the case of a questionable fill (the common term for a completed order), the runner is usually responsible for reporting to the exchange's Time and Sales department to receive a listing of all trade prices between any two designated time periods. The Time and Sales department is the exchange body which keeps the official records of all trades. Disputes over whether a particular transaction could have taken place during a certain time period, say between 10:00 and 10:10 a.m., are resolved by the official records of the Time and Sales department.

**Fetching Lunch and Other Important Stuff:** A runner's other duties are the same as any other low position in a hierarchy, including searching the floor for lost orders, relaying messages, and fetching lunch for the bosses. One runner told me, "Keeping up on the latest baseball stats is my major responsibility."

### Do You Need to Know Anything Special to Read an Order?

Yes, but you'll learn quickly. Reading the orders isn't always easy. Nobody writes an order in longhand. It takes too long. A runner must learn the symbols used for the different commodity months and contracts. A typical order might read: B 10 U US---. Translated, this means buy (B) 10 (10) September (U) United States Treasury Bonds (US) at the best possible current price (---). B and S are used for buy and sell. Each month of the year has a special letter symbol. In addition, each commodity has a special symbol. Commodities and their symbols are shown in the Appendix.

### What Are the Real Benefits of Being a Runner?

Running offers the ambitious young person incomparable opportunities to learn the business. The smartest people use running and other floor jobs as a training ground for their own pit trading. One twenty-eight-year-old millionaire who started as a runner at the CBOT five years ago told me that when he wasn't playing liar's poker (a popular game runners play using the serial numbers on dollar bills as poker hands), he used his free time as a runner to watch one particular trader: "I read his statement every morning and couldn't believe how much money he made every day. During my breaks, I would just stand outside the pit and watch him. He was a spreader. A goddamn machine—disciplined, predictable, and mechanical. But I learned a lot from him and today I trade a lot like him. I hate to admit it, but I used to read everybody's statements. It wasn't right, but I wanted to know how much money everybody was making."

Basically, the job allows you to discover the market for the first time—to see its wild fluctuations, feel its rhythms, sense its turns, learn the players, and understand the stakes. But the best part about being a runner is that it doesn't last very long. If you're smart, no company is going to waste you as a runner for more than a year, except possibly for the large national firms, which often have elaborate floor hierarchies that are difficult to crack in a short time. Most people run for four to nine months before becoming a phone clerk.

### How Can a Runner Screw Up?

Probably the worst mistake a runner can make is to bring an order to the wrong pit. In my first week as a runner, when I was seventeen, I cost my employer over $1000. I brought a 10 lot of corn to the wheat pit, which cost the company $600, and I brought a September bond contract to the December bond broker, which cost the firm another $400.

Of course, everybody screws up sooner or later. You'll hear horror stories of runners whose mistakes have cost their firms over $200,000. [At an average salary of $4 an hour, working six hours a day, five days a week, a runner would have to work about thirty years to pay back that mistake.] Ideally, the broker who fills the order should catch the runners' mistakes, but in the middle of a hectic market, brokers don't have time to read anything on the order except the price, and, as a result, mistakes are common.

### What's the Best Time to Get a Job as a Runner?

First I'll tell you the worst time: May and June. That's when all the firms say thank you to their best customers by hiring those customers' high school and college age sons and daughters as runners for the summer. If you want to get a job, go looking in September after all the summer help has gone back to school. Since the pay is low and the hours relatively short, most runners hold two jobs, either working in the afternoon in the back office of a clearing house or moonlighting at a bar or restaurant.

## PHONE CLERK
### Hours: Market
### Average Salary: $15,000-$500,000

A phone clerk is the next step up the ladder from a runner. The job's major responsibility consists of taking orders from and reporting orders back to customers either over the phone or via telex. The position requires a familiarity with exchange rules, an ability to handle customers, and an understanding of the various market forces. It's hard to pinpoint exactly what a phone clerk does because the term includes everyone from the $15,000-a-year clerk who just answers the phone, to a floor account executive (AE) who has clients, offers them market advice, and can make up to $500,000 a year. In practice, the differences between the responsibilities of a phone clerk and those of an AE usually are insignificant. One twenty-eight-year-old, earning more than $150,000 a year as an AE and who only two years ago was earning just $15,000 as a phone clerk, admitted, "The only difference between being a phone clerk and an AE is how much I make." In addition, different firms allow their clerks different degrees of responsibility. Some firms buy their clerks memberships, which permits the clerk to flash buy and sell signals directly into the pit and some firms permit their clerks to give market advice. But other firms do not want their clerks to be anything more than a robot answering the phone and writing down the customers' orders.

### What Are a Phone Clerk's Responsibilities?

**Answers Phone:** A clerk's day revolves around answering the phones. The phone clerk is always ready to write down customers' orders as quickly as possible. In most professional trading and commercial houses, the phone clerks speak directly to the customers, while in the large, retail houses, an AE serves as the link through whom all orders go before they are sent to the exchange floor from a firm's wire room.

A clerk must enunciate clearly and listen carefully to every customer order. The worst mistake a clerk can make is to misinterpret a customer's order and send the wrong order into the marketplace. Not only is the customer dissatisfied because the order wasn't properly filled, but the phone clerk puts the firm at risk with the mistaken fill. One of the quickest ways to get yourself fired from any firm is to hold onto a mistaken fill, hoping the trade will become profitable, instead of immediately taking your profit or loss. No firm wants a clerk who risks the firm's money while trying to cover up a mistake. Phone clerks should always read the entire order back to the customer to minimize errors. In addition, most firms tape record all phone calls in order to have an audible record of every transaction.

**Time Stamp:** Once an order has been written out, the phone clerk time stamps it and enters it into the market via a runner. The time stamp, which is required by law and prints the date and time to the nearest second, protects both the customer and firm from market fraud. Phone clerks are required to time stamp every order once before they enter it into the market and a second time the instant it returns, thus narrowing down as closely as possible the time period that the order was in the market place. In the case of a questionable fill, the time stamp allows regulatory officials to determine the legitimacy of a particular fill by comparing its price with officially recorded prices during the same time period. For example, if a market order—that is, an order to buy or sell at the best possible price at the moment the order enters the pit—entered the market at 10:06 a.m. and returned at 10:08 a.m. and received a fill at a price above or below those officially recorded by the exchange, then the broker who filled the order must by law adjust the order to fit within the market range.

**Confirm Fill:** Once an order has been filled and returned to the desk via a runner, the phone clerk immediately time stamps it. The clerk then checks the order to see that it has been properly filled. A phone clerk must be careful. It's not uncommon, especially in busy markets, for a broker to misread an order and accidently fill an order that shouldn't have been filled. It's also not uncommon for a broker to receive a better fill than the one specified by the customer on the order. The phone clerk checks to see that the broker has included the proper information to insure a complete order: (1) the name or number of the opposing firm with which the trade was made, (2) the initials of the opposing trader with whom the trade was made, (3) the price at which the trade was made, (4) the quantity, and (5) the broker's identification number. The customer is called, the trade confirmed, and the order is sent to the backoffices where the clearing process begins. More on that later in this chapter.

### Orders: What Are We Really Talking About?

An order consists of six different pieces of information: account number, buy-sell, quantity, month-year, commodity, and type of order. Phone clerks must carefully record each piece of information because an error in any part makes it impossible for an order to be properly filled:

1. *Account Number:* Each customer has at least one account number. For the customers' taxes and for the firm's bookkeeping, it's extremely important that the clerk record the right account number. Moreover, the numbers insure anonymity. Even the brokers who fill their orders don't know the customers' names—only their account numbers.

2. *Buy-Sell:* This piece of information is straightforward and simple to record. There are two choices—you can either buy something or sell something.

3. *Quantity:* This part can cause problems because some commodities are measured by contract size while others are

measured by the number of contracts. For example, grain contracts are measured by the number of bushels. Wheat, corn, and soybeans at the CBOT all have 5,000 bushels to a contract. In placing an order, the customer says the number of bushels he wants to buy or sell (minus the thousands). If a customer wants to buy 5 contracts of corn, he says 25 corn (for 25,000 bushels). In contrast, financial instruments are generally measured by the number of contracts. Even though one contract of swiss franc futures consists of 125,000 swiss francs, a customer should never say he wants to buy 125,000 francs. He should simply say one contract. Phone clerks should not assume that a customer knows this—they should clarify exactly how much a client wants to buy or sell.

4. *Month-Year:* All futures contracts are traded in different months across a number of years. A common error of beginning phone clerks is to assume the year and month about which the customer is speaking. It is particularly common to assume, given the month, that the customer is speaking about the closest year's contract, since the nearest months are by far the most actively traded. But the intelligent phone clerk doesn't assume anything about a customer's intentions. A good clerk always asks for further information.

5. *Commodity:* As mentioned earlier, the most common problem with this instruction is that runners mistakenly bring the order to the wrong pit. Instead of buying 50,000 bushels of soybeans, the customer buys 50,000 bushels of wheat. Usually the error is discovered by the broker but not always. To guard against this, phone clerks often shout out the name of the desired commodity as they hand the order to a runner.

6. *Types of Orders:* Phone clerks must know the different types of orders and the restrictions regarding certain orders at various exchanges. Restrictions on orders have occurred since 1973 as a result of increased levels of trading and price volatility. Orders that could once be handled with relative

ease are no longer allowed because they have become a burden in the marketplace. I have provided a full list and description of orders in the Appendix.

Some of the desciptions are rather technical. Don't worry. It's not necessary to understand every little detail. The list merely offers an example of the type of information a phone clerk must possess and that anyone on the trading floor quickly learns.

### What Are the Real Benefits of Being a Phone Clerk?

Although different firms give their clerks different degrees of independence, almost all phone clerks are asked to be the customers' eyes and ears on the trading floor. At the very least, before entering a trade, most customers want to know the current bids and offers on the floor, the spread prices, the brokerage houses which have been big buyers or sellers, and the general level of market activity. Customers are constantly trying to pick a phone clerk's brain for that little bit of extra information which may give them the trading edge. At best, a customer has a quotation screen in front of him, which in busy markets is at least several trades behind actual market activity. A clerk's official list of responsibilities doesn't include being a market analyst, but, nevertheless, clerks should learn how to judge market strength and weakness and how to relay this to the customers. Just like the traders in and outside the pit, phone clerks must watch key support and resistance levels. To keep a closer eye on these levels, many phone clerks keep daily charts. Phone clerks also learn to keep an eye on the brokers to see at what prices the big buy and sell orders exist. Clerks also watch out for Federal Reserve activity, whose intervention in the market can have a significant effect on prices and about whom customers demand the latest information.

A smart phone clerk will learn from the trading skills of outside customers. The first thing anybody who works for a retail firm should notice is that most of the customers lose money. By asking why they lose, a phone clerk can learn as much from the losers as the winners. The chance to learn from other people's mistakes is one of the chief rewards of working on the floor and particularly as a phone clerk.

I remember one lousy trader but good customer of Goodman-Manaster's who taught me some valuable lessons about risk and reward when I first worked as a phone clerk between my freshman and sophomore years in college. Every morning he either bought or sold 5 US treasury bonds on the opening and took the risk of making 3 ticks on the trade or losing 16 ticks. Each tick is worth $31.25 for each bond contract. For six weeks straight, he made 3 ticks every day, almost $470 per day or $2,350 a week. I saw him make over $20,000 in a couple months. I thought the guy knew something. But after a while, his luck ran out and near the end of the summer, he lost more than $25,000 in three weeks. It was a financial disaster for the man but an education for me. I knew beforehand that the the man's strategy of taking small profits at the risk of big losses was a losing game, but there's nothing quite like seeing the devastating effects to teach you an important lesson. Indeed, that's a large reason working on the floor is so important: you're able to see the real life effects of different trading strategies. The guy was a lousy trader, but he taught me some important lessons free of charge.

Another benefit of working as a phone clerk is the chance to get to know the customers, which often does lead to further job opportunities. Jim, a twenty-seven-year-old trader and broker at the CBOT, became the personal floor broker of a customer he met while he was a phone clerk. Besides receiving the commissions for filling the customer's orders (most brokers receive $1.50 for every lot they fill), the customer's company gave him a membership and a small base salary. Today, he earns over $80,000 a year. Another example is George, who landed his job as a floor account executive courtesy of one of his customers. The client, a huge bond trader, preferred to trade in whatever company George worked for. So in an effort to get the customer's business, another company offered George a job.

For instance is not proof, but Jim and George are just two examples of what happens on the exchange floor. They are not unusual. In an industry growing as fast as commodities, opportunities arise. The trick is being on the floor.

## TRADE CHECKER
### Hours: 3:00–6:00 p.m.
### Average Salary: $125 a week

Trade checking is a part-time job after the close of the market, usually performed by young people who work on the floor during the day as phone clerks, runners, broker's assistants, and trader's assistants. The work can be tedious and it's not as exciting as working on the floor, but for the young person who wants to learn the business, trade checking can be an invaluable step to becoming a first-rate trader. It's also a nice supplementary income. It is not necessary to work for a firm during market hours in order to work for them after the close. Many people work for one firm during the day and another after the close of the market. Typically, a person doesn't become a trade checker right away. It requires a thorough knowledge of the trading process. Most people work as a runner for at least four months before they begin as trade checkers in the afternoon.

### What's a Trade Checker Do?

At the close of each trading day, a brokerage house must report its trades to the exchange's clearing corporation. The trade checker is responsible for insuring that each trade is properly recorded, including the price, quantity, and brokerage house.

### Why Do Brokerage Houses Have to Report Their Orders to the Clearing Corporation?

The clearing corporation is an important part of the structure of all commodity exchanges, but most people out of the industry are unfamiliar with it. It protects the exchange from any financial trouble in the event of bankruptcy by one brokerage house.

When a brokerage firm transacts an order for one of its customers, it accepts the financial responsibility of the trade. The reason? If the customer can't pay his debt, the brokerage firm must meet that customer's financial obligations. But what happens if a brokerage firm goes bankrupt and can't pay off its debts? Who guarantees its financial obligations? The answer: the clearing corporation, which guarantees the fulfillment of each and every trade made at the exchange.

### How Does It Do That?

The clearing corporation acts like a giant link at the exchange by taking the opposite side of every trade made. It transfers the risk of fulfillment from individual brokerage houses, all of which are subject to financial risks, to the clearing corporation, whose finances are backed by the combined forces of all of its member firms. Just as firms act as a link between customers all over the world, making it possible for a farmer in Germany to trade with a widow in Iowa without having to know each other's financial situation or each other, the clearing corporation acts as a middleman between brokerage houses.

For example, say Merrill Lynch buys 5 wheat from Smith-Barney at a specified price at the CBOT. At the end of the day, both firms will report the trade to the clearing corporation. At that point, instead of Merrill Lynch having bought 5 wheat from Smith-Barney, Merrill has actually bought 5 wheat from the clearing corporation and Smith-Barney has actually sold five to it. As a result, the two firms are no longer dependent on each other for the fulfillment of the trades. If one goes bankrupt, the other won't lose anything because the clearing corporation is now responsible for the opposite side of both trades.

### How Is the Clearing Corporation Able to Guarantee Each Trade?

From a pool of money established by its member firms. Each firm is required to post margin deposits with the clearing corporation. If one firm collapses, the collective resources of all the firms guarantees its trades. In truth, the corporation is similar to the Federal Depository Insurance Corporation (FDIC), which eliminates the fear of a bank failure by guaranteeing up to $100,000 individual bank accounts of its member firms.

### How Does the Trade Checker Fit In?

The trade checker is the key person in the clearing process. Throughout the day, as orders are filled, they are sent to brokerage firms' back offices, where keypunchers record each trade—its quantity, price, account number, broker number, opposing firm number—into a data system. The data system is linked electronically to the clearing corporation. At the other end, the clearing corporation tries to match all the trades against each other (the Merrill Lynch buy with the Smith-Barney sell).

In theory, of course, all the trades should match: for every buy there should be a sell. The clearing corporation will only accept trades that have an equal and opposite side. A trade is only legitimate when it has an equal and opposite trade offsetting it. But the trades never match perfectly. Outtrades—trades that do not have an equal and opposite side —often occur.

The trade checker's job is to clear up as many outtrades as possible. After all the trades have been reported, the clearing corporation issues outtrade sheets. These sheets list all the firm's unmatched trades—both those trades which the firm reported making which have no equal and opposite trade to offset it and those trades which other firms have reported making with the firm in question which also have no equal and opposite trade to offset it.

### Why Are There Outtrades?

A few of the hundred different reasons why trades, which have been properly made, come back from the clearing corporation as mismatched follow:

• A trade may have been improperly keypunched into the data system, which transfers the trade to the clearing corporation. The clearing corporation can't possibly know a trade has been mistyped. The result: a mismatched trade.

• A trader or broker may have miswritten a piece of information on the trading card or order, which was then transferred to the clearing corporation. The result: a mismatched trade.

• A trader's card or order may be so sloppily written that it's illegible. The information transferred to the clearing corporation may then be incomplete or wrong. The result: a mismatched trade.

• A trader may forget to turn in a few cards. Cards left in pockets are common. Lost trades occur. The result: a mismatched trade.

It's not necessary to list all the possible errors. The important point is that the trade checker quickly becomes an expert in all of the ways in which mistakes can and do occur in the trading pit. Sometimes, the mistakes are obvious, say, a mistyped quantity by one of the keypunchers. But sometimes the problems are more complicated. A good trade checker has to be familiar with the habits and trading patterns of traders to solve a particular problem quickly.

A trade checker can't always adjust the reported mismatched trades. Real outtrades do occur and they cost traders and brokers millions of dollars a year. One bad outtrade can cost thousands of dollars and destroy months of hard work.

If an outtrade does occur, say, for example, one trader believes he bought 5 bonds at a particular price and the other trader believes he sold only 1 bond, then the two traders must settle the dispute for themselves. This usually happens the following morning before the the market opens. But since most outtrades are an error in communication, the cost is shared by both traders. Occasionally, when an outtrade can't be settled on friendly terms, the dispute is taken to arbitration, where exchange officials settle the dispute.

### What Are the Benefits of Trade Checking?

By itself, of course, trade checking can't teach someone how to trade, but it's excellent preparation before stepping into the pits. It offers the chance to see the trading cards of experienced pit traders and outside customers and to learn some of the trading techniques of the best traders.

Perhaps more important, working in the back office of a firm, learning how a trade is cleared, and correcting outtrades eliminates much of the mystery about the trading process. Many traders who never bothered to work in the back office of a firm don't understand the fundamentals of the clearing process. This may be reflected in their trading abilities. But for a young person who has the time and desire, the experience of working as a trade checker is worth it, if only to eliminate any questions about where, what, and how a trade is cleared.

The job also drills an important lesson into any trade checker's head: guard against outtrades—they can cost hundreds of thousands of dollars. Some of the biggest outtrades easily could have been avoided if the simple precaution of checking every trade had been taken. The trade checker learns this lesson well.

## MORNING OUTTRADE CLERK
### Hours: 6:00–8:00 a.m.
### (Changes according to different markets)
### Average Salary: $125 a week

Another floor job closely linked to the trade checker is the outtrade clerk. The outtrade clerk works in the morning before the market opens. He or she is responsible for alerting a firm's customers of their outtrades. An outtrade clerk is not a full-time job. It's strictly a morning job, just like trade checking is an afternoon job. Most outtrade clerks work on the floor during the day as phone clerks and trader's assistants. They work as an outtrade clerk in the morning to earn a little extra money and learn still another aspect of the floor operations.

## FLOOR MANAGER
### Hours: Market Hours
### Average Salary: $30,000-$60,000

The floor manager is the highest floor position in most firms. He or she is responsible for overseeing the smooth running of all floor operations and for insuring customer satisfaction. Complaints from both employees and customers are directed to the floor manager. The job requires good organizational and management skills, as well as a thorough knowledge of the exchange.

### *What Are the Floor Manager's Responsibilities?*

**Customer Complaints:** The most time consuming responsibility of most floor managers is handling customer complaints. Three-quarters of an average floor manager's time is spent on customers' problems. The complaints range from petty gripes about customer service to serious accusations of market fraud.

The most common problem is adjusting customers' profit and loss statements. The profit and loss statement is the daily update of a customer's account, including the previous day's trades, open positions, current balance, and commission fees. A day rarely goes by when all the firm's statements are accurate. A typical problem might involve a corn trader whose statement mistakenly showed him losing $3,000. It's the floor manager's job to correct the problem by reviewing each of the trader's previous day's trades. These errors usually are the result of a trade having been placed in the wrong account and, with a little detective work, they are easily corrected.

**Payroll and Hours:** The floor manager also oversees the payroll and work schedule. Among other things, the floor manager must insure that each order desk has enough phone clerks and runners to handle the business. Most firms have several desks at a large exchange. At the CBOT, for example, the firm I worked for had three desks: one desk for grains, one for financial futures, and one for stock index futures. In addition, many floor managers keep the payroll records: attendance, hours, overtime.

### What Are the Real Benefits of
### Being a Floor Manager?

This job is different from the others I've described. By the time a person becomes a floor manager, he or she has already worked for several years as a runner, phone clerk, and trade checker and knows the ins and outs of the industry. The job is a managerial position, and many floor managers are satisfied company employees who have no interest in trading for themselves. Other floor managers use the position to build capital before they begin trading. In other words, the job is not a critical step in learning the business. A floor manager already knows the business. The job is often a career in itself.

## MARGIN CLERK
### Hours: 9:00 a.m.–5:00 p.m.
### Average Salary: $17,000–$30,000

A backdoor to the floor of any exchange is working as a margin clerk for a brokerage firm. These jobs don't put you directly on the exchange floor, and therefore are not ideal for learning trading skills and acquiring a good market sense, but they can lead to a floor position. The job demands a lot of financial paper work and finance skills, but doesn't ordinarily require an MBA or other special degree.

### What Are the Responsibilities of a Margin Clerk?

The job of a margin clerk is to insure the firm's financial security. This can be broken down into three main areas.

**Screening Applicants:** Brokerage houses won't just take any customer who comes to them and wants to open an account. They assess the financial risk of the customer by reviewing his or her personal financial condition, past trading record, and stated trading objectives. Formal records reveal some of this information, but most margin departments go beyond the mere formalities in assessing a customer's risk. A margin department may call brokerage houses through which the customer has traded, make inquiries about the applicant to friends, or may interview the applicant several times. Different firms take varying degrees of precautions, but since each firm is legally responsible for its customer's trades, a critical review of every applicant protects the firm.

**Monitoring Positions:** Following each trading day, a margin clerk reviews each customer's profit and loss statement. The clerk is concerned primarily with the overall financial position of the account and not in a particular day's profit or loss. Specifically, a clerk reviews each account to check for margin and debit calls. A margin call occurs when a customer carries too large a position in his or her account in relation to the amount of cash in the account. Each account is required by law to have a certain amount of cash, called margin, for each commodity carried in the account. For example, every US treasury bond that a speculator buys or sells must be backed by $2000 in the speculator's account. The exchanges themselves determine specific margin requirements, but individual firms may require more. A person has five days to respond to a margin call. A debit call occurs when an individual account has an overall debit. A person usually has only one day to respond to a debit call.

**Recommending Preventive Medicine:** Part of a margin clerk's responsibilty is to foresee trouble before it comes. A clerk is always checking accounts for unusual occurrences: an account which has slowly but steadily been losing money; a small trader who suddenly begins trading in increasingly larger quantities; or a day trader who starts holding positions overnight. None of these cases guarantees a financial disaster, but they are all signs that a customer may become a financial risk in the future.

### What Are the Real Problems of Working As a Margin Clerk?

Anybody who is serious about becoming a floor trader would do well to get out from the back office as soon as possible. You'll learn a lot about the business, but if you spend your time off the floor, you can't watch the experienced traders or acquire a feel for the market—a high a price to pay for someone who wants to be a trader. In short, working as a margin clerk is a roundabout way to the trading floor. Better you should be a runner.

### BROKER'S ASSISTANT and TRADER'S ASSISTANT
#### Hours: Market Hours
#### Average Salary: $8,000-$30,000

Both of these jobs are excellent ways to enter the industry. They offer distinct advantages over the more common route of working for a brokerage firm. Unfortunately, these jobs are more difficult to get. It's about as easy to walk in and become a trader's assistant as it is to become a bat-boy for a professional baseball team. For these jobs it's not what you know; it's who you know. Usually, it's only after you've made friends and proved your competence that a broker or trader will hire you.

### What Are the Responsibilities of a Trader's Assistant?

Obviously, each trader treats an assistant differently but the job entails five major responsibilities:

**Counting Cards:** The assistant keeps track of the trader's changing position in the market by counting trading cards. For example, a trader may have bought 39 bonds and sold 45. It's the clerk's responsibilty to tell the trader that he or she is short 6 bonds—that is, the trader sold 6 more than have been bought. Traders also want to know at what price they are long or short.

**Clarifying Cards:** In the middle of a busy market, most traders don't take the time to write neatly. This can cause problems later in the day when the trades are cleared. The trader's assistant makes sure the cards are legible and the information is correct, including the price, the commodity symbol, the initials, and the time-bracket in which the trade occurred.

**Checking Trades:** In order to avoid outtrades, the assistant checks the trades with other traders and brokers assistants, making sure that both sides agree about exactly what the trade specifications are—size, price, commodity.

**Preparing Statements:** Many assistants are responsible for getting the trader's statement in the morning, so that the trader knows his or her financial standing and current market position.

**Checking Outtrades:** Also in the morning, some assistants check with the outtrade clerk to see if the trader has any outtrades from the previous day.

### What Are the Responsibilities of a Broker's Assistant?

A broker's assistant has three major responsibilities:

**Relaying Orders:** A broker's assistant stands behind the broker and watches the order desks of the broker's clients. Most orders are flashed into the pit by hand signals. The assistant, acting as a relay, sees the signals and then tells the broker exactly what to do.

**Counting Fills:** After the broker has filled an order, the assistant double checks the fill by counting to make sure the proper number of contracts were filled. Filling a one lot isn't a problem, but many brokers are doing hundred and thousand lots.

**Transcribing Fills:** Most broker's assistants write the fills from the broker's cards on to the order itself. If a broker fills an order to buy 100 Swiss Francs, the chances are good that the trade was made with several different traders and, maybe, at two different prices. Most brokers find it easier to write their fills on a card and then hand the card to the assistant, who takes the information from the card and then writes it out on the actual order.

### What Are the Advantages of Being a Broker's Assistant/Trader's Assistant?

The best way to become a broker is to make connections. One way to do this is to work for a broker. As futures have grown, so has the individual broker's business. Most brokers need someone to help fill their orders. Brokers typically give their assistants the smaller orders to fill, either buying them memberships or loaning them money to buy their memberships. Gradually, the smaller orders grow larger and larger and, in a matter of time, the former assistants have their own clients and their own assistants.

The advantage of being a trader's assistant is the chance to get in close with a trader who can teach you trading strategies and, even better, help you financially when the times come to get into the pit.

But working for a trader isn't necessarily the best route to becoming one. I asked one trader what he thought, and he said, "I highly recommend the job for anyone who can count to ten." He felt that a young person who wants to become a trader may learn more working for a firm and watching the outside customers. This gives a broader picture of the floor operations. But, beyond question, a young person who wants to become a broker should work for a broker.

### What About Exchange Jobs?

A final way to enter the industry is as an employee of the exchange. But be careful: It's the least desirable way to enter the business for someone interested in a career on the floor. And not all the jobs are equally rewarding. In fact, except for one or two, most of the jobs are a waste of time for someone interested in becoming a trader or floor broker.

### INVESTIGATOR: OFFICE OF INVESTIGATIONS
#### Hours: 9 a.m.–5 p.m.
#### Average Salary: $17,000-$30,000

The Office of Investigations is mainly responsible for enforcing the Commodity Futures Trading Commission (CFTC) rules regarding exchange trading. Most of an investigator's day is spent handling referrals—that's the fancy word for complaints—from outside customers, member traders, member firms, and employees of firms.

A typical complaint from an outside customer may concern a bad fill or an "unable"—that is, an order that can't be filled at the specified price. A common complaint from a floor trader is the accusation of prearranged trades—that is, the charge that a broker and trader are in collusion with one another and that the orders are not being properly filled in an open outcry market. Still another accusation is that a broker is trading in front of his orders—that is, a broker who, knowing the orders in his deck, takes advantage of this information to trade for himself first before he trades for his client.

A typical investigation involves reconstructing the trading activity at the time the complaint in question occurred. The investigator can review any and all documents of a brokerage firm. It has complete access to the information of the Clearing Corporation. The investigator conducts interviews with the people involved—from runner to phone clerk to officers of a firm and legal staff.

Becoming an investigator in the Office of Investigations is probably the best preparation of any exchange job for a floor career. An investigator is involved in floor operations, has access to traders, and must be fully versed in different trading strategies and techniques. Unlike other exchange jobs, an investigator is exposed to all the various exchange operations.

One of the best parts of the jobs is access to traders. The investigator doesn't always have an adversial relationship with the trader. It's often one of mutual education. In the process of an investigation, an investigator has the chance to learn firsthand the trading strategies of different traders— sometimes receiving private lessons, as it were, about why and how traders do certain things.

Unlike floor jobs, a college degree, with emphasis in finance or business, is required to work as an investigator.

### QUOTATIONS CLERK
#### Hours: Market Hours
#### Average Salary: $12,000-$15,000

Another exchange job that gives you access to the floor is work as a quotations clerk. The quotations clerk sits by the side of the pit and is responsible for punching up the changing prices to the quotations boards and the ticker-tape. It's a tedious and low paying job, but it offers the chance to be on the exchange floor, to make connections, and to observe the markets.

### How About Other Opportunities?

The exchanges, particularly the larger ones, also offer a wide selection of excellent career opportunities that are far removed from actual floor operations. I've listed a few here:

**Public Relations:** Like any other large company, the exchange tries to maintain amiable relations with the press and the general public. The public relations department provides information for the public, and maintains a visitors' center.

**Information System:** The fluid flow of information is the lifeblood of an exchange. When the quotations boards break down, trading ceases. Today's exchanges are almost completely computerized and are continually updating their systems to achieve the fastest and most efficient exchange of information. Systems analysts, programmers, and telecommunications experts are needed by every exchange.

**Educational Services:** Most exchanges house small libraries devoted to futures-related subjects. This department also conducts orientation programs and mandatory testing of new members, as well as coordinating educational programs with local colleges and high schools to increase understanding of futures.

**Audits:** In compliance with CFTC regulations, the exchanges keep close watch of the financial operations of individual firms. They conduct routine and surprise audits on member firms, insuring that all firms are properly capitalized. Accounting degrees are required.

**Marketing:** This department is usually more closely involved in actual floor dealings than most of the others. Its major responsibility is the planning and promoting of new exchange contracts. The department promotes new contracts through seminars, literature, and personal contacts. The success of any new contract depends on the proper market participants understanding the new contract. The introduction of a new contract, say options on corn futures, involves hundreds of meetings with commodity brokers, farmers, and large grain companies.

Whether you want to jump into the trading pit or stay on the periphery, I think the job descriptions I've given in this chapter will get you started in the right direction.

# 3

## The Voices of Young Traders

The voices in this chapter represent the young and hungry people at the exchanges who hope to be the millionaires of the future. Looking through a variety of career books, I noticed that it's common to interview the most famous and well-established people in a profession and use them as models for success. Interested in a career in broadcasting? Well Howard Cosell says this. Or how about a career in modelling? Cheryl Tiegs says . . .

It may sell books to interview Howard Cosell, but I don't think the stars can offer as timely and practical advice to a young person who wants to enter a particular profession as the voices of other young people already in the industry. The people who tell their stories in this chapter have just gone through or are still going through the process of becoming traders and brokers. You can feel the frustration and pain in their voices. They know what's going on because they're right in the middle of it. And their stories are real. Usually, by the time someone reaches the top in a particular field, the past has been thoroughly mythologized. Not so here.

The ten young men and women interviewed here are a diverse lot. Five are traders. One is a broker's assistant, one a trader's assistant, one is a floor account executive, one just handed her arbitrage business to someone else while she examines her *career* options, and another is vice-president of a clearing house. Of the five who are traders, one is also a part-time broker, another trades for a company, and three trade for themselves. And they are not all "successful." The most financially successful among them is the floor account executive. Three of the traders have shown themselves to be consistent money-makers and two are still struggling.

Connections? One of them had a father in the business and two of them had brothers. But the other seven had no relations, just friends and acquaintances, who in some cases helped them land a job but in most simply encouraged them to start looking for one themselves.

Some common denominators among them:

1. They're all college graduates, and two of them have MBAs. There's no doubt about it: the competition for jobs is growing. In the past, a college degree wasn't very important, and it's still not absolutely necessary, but when a brokerage firm has the choice between a college grad and a high school drop-out, they'll usually choose the college graduate.

2. Of the traders, only one paid for her membership outright. I've devoted a whole chapter to how to obtain a membership without buying one (see chapter 4). It is a rare young person who has the money to buy or even rent a membership. Even the cheapest memberships at the larger exchanges cost $25,000. Most of the new traders receive help from wealthy traders in the pit.

3. The same phrases keep coming up in each interview. Phrases like "I was in the right place at the right time," "I caught a lucky break," "I was just in a real fortunate position," and "I got lucky." But the truth is none of these people was lucky. What they call luck is really part of the benefit of working on the floor. In an industry growing as fast as commodities, opportunities arise. These people took advantage of those opportunities.

They disagree with one another about what's important. One of them thinks "trade checking is important before you begin trading" and another calls it "bulls‑‑‑." One of them says that "no one really needs a book like this." And, who knows, for some people that may be true. But they are honest, and the advice they give is worth reading. Their names, and often the names of the firms they've worked at, have been changed to help them feel uninhibited. I think you'll agree that they did.

## *Steve*

"I never thought I'd be in the business. I always thought that in order to be in the business, you had to have a rich family, or have a father in the business, or have another connection. Of course I knew about the business because, first, I grew up on the North Shore and knew a lot of families in the business and, second, a lot of my friends during high school were runners. At the time, I thought that they were just wasting their time, passing away the summer. Now, the bottom line is I wish I had done that during high school. Not that I'd be a better trader. I just would have been better connected, and I think I would have felt more comfortable down here. You know, once you're down here, you hear all the stories about the big guys like Lee Stern and Hank Shatkin who started out in the mail room and s——— like that. Well, it doesn't always happen that way, but a lot of it's true."

*Steve, twenty-four, graduated from the University of Arizona in May 1983. He began working as a clerk in August 1983 at the Chicago Board of Options Exchange (CBOE) for a big independent trader. After a year, his boss set him up to trade at the Chicago Board of Trade (CBOT) in what was then the newest stock index futures contract, the Major Market Index (MMI). After one year of trading, Steve says, "I'm even. I haven't lost any money, but I haven't made any money either." It's still a question whether Steve can succeed in the pits, but he's determined and says, "I'll be there as long as my money is there."*

"But the older I got, the more and more I heard about people my age trading. I thought, 'S———, if they can do it, I can do it.' Total idiots I knew from high school were down here trading. Don't laugh. I figured that if they could do it, I could do it, too.

"After I tried every connection I had, I finally got a job in a roundabout way. My brother knew a guy who knew a guy who needed a clerk on the floor of the CBOE. So I hooked up with him.

"Basically, I would do all the things that he used to do for himself when he was younger and couldn't afford to hire someone. In the morning, I would go down there and put all of his positions on a card, his long and shorts, and how much stock he had. I'd check all his outtrades, confirm his trades. That kind of stuff. It was bulls——— work, but it didn't suck because you need to know it. You need to know how to read the statements; you need to know what your short interest is; you need to know what trade equity is.

"How much was I making? $800 a month, clearing $319 every two weeks. My train pass costs me $100 a month. God forbid I should get a date or go out with somebody! It's tough to live on what they pay you. You think about college, and it was easy to live on that much a month. God, if you had that much a month, you were King of the Road.

"But I knew I was in a great position. I mean, here I am working for this guy who is nice, who is loaded, who is smart, and who is successful. You know, when I first came down on the floor, all I wanted to be was a runner. But I got lucky to get with him. I would have had to work myself up to a phone clerk or a stock clerk in a crowd of people. But I was there with him. Guys would have worked for free to do what I did—to stand behind some guy, get along with him, and hope they get set up with him. In fact, when I left the guy, they were all dying for my old job. I just got into a good thing.

"About the eighth or ninth month, you start getting really edgy. If you're sharp, there's only so much you can learn and only so much bulls——you can take until you want to move in and start doing things for yourself. But I didn't want to go up and ask him, 'Hey, are you going to set me up?' You just don't do that. It's like saying, 'Hey, are you going to give me money or not?' It's not right. He'll back you when he thinks you're ready. It's up to him.

"Well, everything worked out. In July, he said I would work for him—trade for him and be his partner, with one other guy. He and another guy had decided to back me financially, just like I hoped, and I'd split my trading profits with them. But at the time they gave me the offer, the CBOE was dying; it was going through one of those cycles when there was just no business, seat rents were high, and no paper was going through. That's really not the place for a young trader to start and build some confidence. So, this new contract was starting at the Board of Trade, the MMI, which was a stock index future, so everything I learned at the options about reading the tape and about equities would be applicable there. It wouldn't be like stepping into the corn or soybean pit—stuff I didn't know anything about.

"They each put $2,500 in my account, a total of $5,000. And here I am moving up to become a trader, thinking, 'OK I'm gonna make $1,000 or $2,000 a month salary.' But I made less. My base salary dropped to $600 a month. But, of course, if I could make $1,000 a day, I'd get $500 of it; or $500 a day, I'd get $250. They also said that if I made money and wanted to leave—no problem. I could leave any time. They were really cool about it. They were thinking, 'We'll risk $2,500 each, and if this kid's good and sharp, maybe he'll make us a lot of money. What do we have to lose but $2,500. Besides, we're helping him out.'

"As it turned out, I got into the pit and found it very difficult. Scalping commodities is much more difficult than option spreads. The guys who set up people in the options can literally walk you through the whole thing. They take you by the hand and tell you exactly what to do. It's a much slower game over there. But here, I was on my own. Everything I did was my own shot. There was nobody holding my hand.

"The first four months I lost $1,000 trading. Which I didn't think was too bad. But at the end of four months on Jan. 1, 1985, the guys came back to me and said, 'Here's the deal. You can either continue working for us and trade the

MMI, but you'll take no salary and no percentage of profits until you get back the $5,000, or you can come back to the Options Exchange and work.' Well, I thought that was b----- --. So I went on my own. The clearing firm let me start with $5,000 in my account. I think I borrowed $1,000 from my brother, and I came up with the rest on my own. And that's where I stand. I've been on my own ever since.

"Sure, they lost all $5,000, but only $1,000 was due to my trading. The rest was salary, and seat rent, and exchange fees.

"The truth is my old boss really set me up well. He wanted me to succeed in the business. He was a real non-believer in partnerships. He only set me up in a partnership to get me going. He says that most of them are bad deals. If you're the junior partner, maybe making $50,000, the other guy's yanking $20,000 or $30,000 at a crack from your account, and you can't say anything because you're working for him. He says a lot of times the agreements aren't really solid. When you're making money, it's great; but when you're losing, you're out. They'll just screw you—sometimes without giving you too much chance. He says the best way to be in this business is to be on your own. Then you don't have to answer to anybody. You don't have to argue with anybody. And your decisions are your own.

"He even put the seat in my name, so I was the owner of the seat. That way I didn't have to have $25,000 in margin. The Commodity Futures Trading Commission (CFTC) makes you have $25,000 in T-bills as collateral to guarantee your trade. But if you own your own seat, then they let you use the value of your seat as collateral. So basically, he just put the seat in my name. He still owned it, of course, and I paid him $150 a month as rent fee, but it's in my name, and I have all membership rights. If I ever want out of the business, I can just sign him back his seat. It's good. I'm not held to any bank or any clearing firm. I don't have any loans. I guess you could say, I'm beating the system a little bit by not having to worry about actually buying a seat or having to come up with the $25,000 to trade. It's a good deal. I think he'd really like to see me do well.

"There's a lot of guys down here in my situation. I'd say over 60 percent of the people in my pit are guys in my shoes—young guys, with limited capital, who want to get into the business. They've heard that you can make a lot of money, or just a good living, or even just $100 or $200 a day, which is fifty grand a year—more than your average Kirkland-and-Ellis, Jenner-and-Block-guy is making, and those guys go to Harvard and Yale. So 60 percent of the guys are beating their heads against the wall like me. And 25 percent of the guys in the pit are brokers, who have no risk. They just fill their orders—most of the time between one another—and little guys like me get crushed in the pit. And the brokers really don't give a s––– what happens. Some of them are nice, but most of them just want to fill their orders and get their $1.50 a shot. And the other 15 percent are the big shooters who make all the money.

"It's hard to say how I'll eventually do, but I'm going to stick it out, and I'll be there as long as my money is there. I like the business a lot. If I ever blow out, I would definitely try to find another way to get either more money or work with someone because I don't want to give up on it. Not to be conceited—I have no right to be—if there's one thing trading is, it's humbling—but I think I'm sharper than a lot of these guys down here. I see a lot of people down here who I don't think belong here, but, then, maybe I don't belong here. I'm big. I'm aggressive. If I could get a little confidence behind me, then, I think, maybe, I can make it.

"A lot of the time I stand in the pit and wonder, 'Is this what I want to do?' But everybody says you've got to give it a year. If you can survive in the pits for a year, then you should be able to do all right in the business. So I'm thinking to myself, 'Well, it's already been nine or ten months. And I'm not doing badly. I'm even.'

"When I have a good two or three weeks, maybe make two

grand, I think, 'Hey, this is a great business. I'm just turning the corner. I'm on my way to making $800 a week.' But, then, boom! You have a couple of s----- weeks. You lose the money you made. Not because you took bigger risks or traded bigger, but because the business just eats you away. It's a grind—a real grind. So one week you're on a high, but two weeks later, you're moping around, saying is this what I want to do? Am I ever going to be successful down here? Maybe I should just sell insurance or work in a real estate office, making my $18-20-22-24,000 a year, and by the time I'm thirty, making $30,000 a year.

"I remember one day I walked by some construction workers behind the Board of Trade. I said to myself that these guys in hard hats are probably making $14-18 an hour and they're top in their business. Even lawyers I've talked to have told me that, sure, they may have billed out for the firm at $100 an hour, but after tax, their net pay is between $15-20 an hour—$20 for the top young lawyers and $12-15 for the rest. And these guys have prestigious degrees.

"I figure, what the hell? These construction guys are making $15 an hour. That's 1 tick on a 1 lot. How can I not make 1 tick on a 1 lot every hour I'm down there? How can I not do that? One tick an hour. How hard is that? It's hard. It doesn't sound hard even to me, but it is. But I can do it. I know I can do that. I guess I've just got to figure out a way to do it. And if I can do it, I'd be making $100 a day. How can I not buy at 1/2 and sell at 5/8 one time every hour every day? It's better than waking up at six a.m. to work construction in the middle of winter. One hundred or two hundred dollars a day is a great living. Think about it. And God forbid, you should get hot and catch a fast market and, maybe, one day you should make $1,000. Who knows what might happen? And that's what keeps me going.

"If I make nothing after two years, I don't know what I'll do. Right now, I'm kind of treating this like graduate school. All my friends are in law school or graduate school, anyway.

The first year is just getting there, getting in the business. The second year you begin trading. Besides, no one said it was easy, and everyone says it takes time. No one's successful right away.

"You have to take a shot when you're young, when you have no mortgage, kids, wife, liabilities, or anything, except living expenses. If I have to live at home for three years because I don't make anything, well, most of my friends will still be in school. Then, all of a sudden, the fourth year I may start making $25,000-35,000. Who knows how much?

"Is it worth it? Hell yes. To me, it's worth it. I don't want to work myself up some corporate ladder. Sure, that's secure. I'd make $18-20-22,000 a year. I wouldn't have to worry about security. But when I'm older, I know I would say, 'I wish I had gone to the markets and tried my hand in commodities.' But it's too hard to go down here when you're older. What are you gonna be a twenty-seven-year-old runner? I'd rather do it now when I'm still a cocky, young simp out of college than I would later coming out of some company like IBM. I don't know if it will work out. I hope it works out. It better work out."

# *Mary*

"You want to know how lost I was? I went to eight different colleges before I graduated. I started off studying the sciences, went into physical therapy, and ended up majoring in business. In between, I studied accounting, but I knew I didn't want to be an accountant. I started at Pierce College in California. Have you ever heard of that? No. Of course not. I graduated from Kean College in New Jersey. Have you ever heard of that? I went to school in Israel, too. After college, I taught tennis at, probably, six different clubs in Jersey, and then I taught at Fort Washington, which is probably the hottest tennis academy on the East Coast. The person who owns Fort Washington happens to be a distant relative of mine. I worked there for a short time and thought, 'I can't stand it!' I was teaching six-year-olds, and I had a constant headache."

*Mary, twenty-eight, the first female arbitrageur to own her own firm on the New York Futures Exchange, began work at the NYFE in 1982 as a clerk. After six months, she began work as an arbitrageur, trading the NYFE's New York Stock Exchange Index and the Chicago Mercantile's S & P Index, working for a local floor trader. Eight months later, she began her own trading company. In her first year, she earned over $100,000. Her second year was slightly less profitable. At the time of this interview, she was out of the arbitrage business. As she says, "The simple arbitrage I was doing was becoming overly saturated. Something like that doesn't last long." She retains her membership on the NYFE.*

"So I stopped teaching, and I felt completely lost. I had no idea what I wanted to do. It was very disturbing. My family is full of doctors: my dad's a psychiatrist, my step-father's an ophthalmologist, my brother's a doctor, my sister's in medical school, my uncle's a doctor, but I kept thinking:

What can I do? What can I be good at? I knew I had some talent. I just didn't know in what area.

"It's a crazy coincidence how I got into this business. I worked some production jobs first, with producers in music and photography. I did some bookkeeping. I didn't last very long in any of these jobs. I was working with professional people, and I just didn't see any future for me in any of those areas. Next, I got a job with Delta working reservations. I wanted to see what the corporate world was like. Delta is *very* corporate. They must have had people from the army, navy, and marines put it together: they monitor your phone calls; they check how long you are on the phone with each customer. They had the Delta way of saying things; and if you were a minute late for work, they would write it down in a book. After six months, I realized this was not for me. It would take me five years to even move up. I didn't even want to stay in that area. I wanted to move to marketing, and *everybody* wants to be in marketing.

"It was Father's day '82. I met some guy who was selling sweaters in a store—I was buying my a father a sweater for Father's day—and we became good friends. He introduced me to his friend Michael, who I ended up going out with, and his roommate—Alan—was a trader on the NYFE. Finally, one day I was totally fed up. I came to Alan and said, 'I can't stand what I'm doing. I don't even know what you do, but I've got to get out of this business.' He was great. He said, 'Alright Mary, I'll hire you. If it doesn't work out, my father will hire you to work for him in his investment banking firm, but you're guaranteed a job.' Nice guy, huh?

"So I went down to the NYFE, and I worked as a runner and trade checker for three other guys and Alan—all young guys, all making good money, ranging in age from twenty-two and twenty-three to Alan who was twenty-five, two years younger than me. These guys were lunatics. They were kids going crazy with the money they were making. They were making thousands of dollars during the day, and blowing it on girls and drugs at night. One of them went out with a girl one time, bought her a $400 leather jacket, and never saw her again. Money meant nothing to them, which I resented because, although they were bright, they just didn't understand what money meant. They're not doing nearly so well today. They paid me well, though. I earned over $300 a week, and I picked up an extra $2,000 at Christmas time.

"One thing I like about the market is you're dealing with a totally mixed breed of people. You've got Jewish, Irish, and Italian people—middle class, upper class, and lower class people. You find everything down there. It's not an exclusive place. Plus you see the people who are really aggressive and want to succeed. You can see the difference between the hungry ones and the complacent ones. You see the girls who go down there and just want to marry rich. They see a broker or a trader who's making a lot of money, and they want to get their hands all over him. Which is funny to me because I never felt that way. I didn't care about watching anybody else make money. I wanted to do it myself.

"After about six months, a trader approached me. He wanted to do an arbitrage between the NYFE's stock index contract and the Chicago Mercantile's S & P's contract. He interviewed me for the job, and hired me after one interview. 'O.K., you're hired,' he said. I panicked. I knew nothing about it. Arbitrage? Are you kidding? I had been down there six months, but I still didn't know the hand signals. He had to teach them to me on the exchange stairway. He paid me $300 a week, plus 15 percent of the first $100,000, 20 percent of the second $100,000, and 25 percent of the third $100,000. I soon learned that with the kind of size he was trading, there was no way we could ever make $300,000. If I were trading the same markets today, with what I know now, I would have made a lot more money. The markets were fantastic back then—not nearly as tight as today and more volatile. But the best part was that he was a great teacher, and he gave me a shot.

"I worked for him for eight months, and then I decided to go it alone, with a partner. I wanted the best broker on the floor to be my partner. The key to a successful arb is fast fills. I wanted somebody to get me filled before anybody else. One guy, Michael, had probably the highest voice in the pit. He was a singer, and his voice was piercing—about ten octaves higher than mine. Everyone heard him first. So I approached him, offered him the chance to be my partner, explained that I wouldn't pay him brokerage, but we would split the trading profits 50-50. Actually, I got a better deal because I got a salary out of it, too. He made good money. But, then he started to take advantage of the deal by not showing up. That meant I had to go through another broker, which meant I had to pay out brokerage. So while he was on vacation, I might be earning $1,000 in a day. That meant he was getting $500 and doing nothing, while I was getting all the headaches. After six months, I broke off that relationship and went totally on my own.

"I went out to Chicago, hired a personal clerk, and selected a broker. I needed a broker who was quick. What I really wanted was a young, aggressive guy, who was really hurting and hungry, who wanted the business bad. Once they start getting the business and the money's coming in, they couldn't care less about you. They start filling you badly, and they start taking vacations. And then when they lose some business, they get aggressive again and start working harder.

"I made money because I was consistent and conservative. Listen, the best kinds of traders are mostly ex-athletes—people who are very quick, have good gut instincts. They'll make a move, but if they make the wrong move, they'll get out fast—very fast. I was a tennis player for ten years. In the eighteen and under, I was ranked number one in Jersey, number eighteen on the East Coast, and number four in California. And it helped. It's a business that's very greedy. You're dealing with ambition and self-interest. Every person out there is out for himself ultimately. You really learn who your friends are. If you get hurt on something and someone comes up to you to help you, but they're not getting hurt, don't think they're your friend.

"I was the sloppiest dresser down there. I never wanted people to know how much I was making by the way I dressed. A lot of people feel that if they dress looking successful, everyone is going to treat them that way. That makes me laugh, but it's true if you're in a corporation. People would crack on me for the way I'd dress. I'd wear cords, sneakers, and a Lacost shirt. I wanted to be comfortable. The floor is such a horrendous place to work, with all the screaming, shouting, and perspiring. I wasn't about to get decked out. I didn't want to put on a $200-300 suit and have somebody come running by with a pen and mark it up. It's not like you're working in an air-conditioned office.

"I'm a jock. I've always interacted well with men, but I never tried to compete with them directly—never tried to intentionally embarrass or hurt one of them. It's kind of a game: compete and yet don't be too obvious about it. I never let anyone know how much I'm making, and I don't want to know what other people are making. I never want to pressure them. I always tried to be a *mensch.* Even to the guys I didn't like, I never wanted anything bad to happen. To be successful in this business, you need friends.

"I tried to get along with everybody. It's very important in this business because if you have a bad name, if people don't like you, if they even *think* you're a crook, they won't trade with you, they won't even take your business. If you're clearing small sizes like I was, you're in no position to hurt anyone by taking away your paper. I was a small local arbitrageur. Yes, I was the first female arbitrageur to own her own business between the NYFE and the Merc, but I was still small.

"There are some guys who don't want women down there. There was one guy—another arbitrageur—who gave me a lot of trouble. If I saw this guy make a good trade, I'd tell him it was a good trade, and everytime he'd give me the dirtiest look and say, 'Don't tell me I just made a good trade. I know if I made a good trade or not.' He was very egotistical. Later, he gave another female a hard time. He pushed her out of her position. I guess the guy just had a problem with women. There are a lot of men like him. I guess they think the floor is not meant for women. I have my ways of dealing. I just try to stay away from guys like that. Else, if someone is really antisocial and aggressive, I find their friends and become friends with them.

"There's a lot of sexual frustration down there. The pressure and anxiety of the pit raises people's sexual energy. A lot of people relieve their tensions sexually. I won't describe it, but the language in the pit is very sexual, too. The pit is filled with the male ego. It's a very raw feeling—raw capitalism, raw human nature.

"I'm in flux now. I gave my clerk and business to someone else. As I see it, I have three options. One, work for an investment house—a Shearson, Drexel, or Goldman, Sachs. But, really, I've got too much experience to work for them at an introductory level. Two, set up my own trading company. It would be challenging and frightening and risky, but I know some smart young guy who, although he doesn't know anything about trading, could set up any kind of trading model I asked for. I'd have to pull together the right people—a computer programmer, experienced traders—and it may flop, but at least I'd flop gracefully—doing something interesting. The third option, which is a compromise between the two, is to work for a small trading company. I could learn about their computer models, their strategies, and work with a team of people, which I enjoy doing."

# *George*

"I felt like an idiot. I had an MBA from Notre Dame, and here I was making $110 a week as a runner! But down here it's like hazing in a fraternity. If anyone comes in and earns a decent salary, everyone thinks he's just sliding by. There's a real feeling down here that you have to pay your dues. I'm sure there were other MBA's on the floor. There's no other way to start. I might have felt stupid, but I also realized that no one was gonna pay me $25,000 a year to run orders into a pit. But even though you realized it, it's still embarrassing visiting your MBA friends the following year at a football game and when they ask you what you're doing, you tell them you make $110 a week as a runner at the Board of Trade."

*George, 28, graduated from John Carroll University in 1978 with a finance major. He immediately went on to receive his MBA from the University of Notre Dame as a way, he says, "to avoid dealing with getting a job rather than out of any strong desire to further my education." After graduating from Notre Dame, he worked in Chicago for Merrill Lynch as a retail broker for eight months before deciding to go to the Board of Trade. He began work at the Board in June 1981 as a runner for a small firm. In six months, he worked himself up to the head phone clerk in the bond room. He quit that job in August 1982 to become a floor account executive for Conti Commodities, which was later bought out by Refco. When interviewed, George was a floor account executive for Refco Financial, earning over $150,000 a year. He says that he came down to the exchange hoping to become a trader, but it soon became clear to him that "there are a lot of other ways to make money down here than just being a trader or floor broker."*

"I worked for Merrill Lynch for eight months, but I hated it there. Being a stock broker is a lot less glamorous than it sounds. It's a lot of long, hard hours, which I didn't like. They just hand you a phonebook and a phone and, maybe, a special list of names and tell you to go call them and convince them that you're the reason why they should trade stocks. About eight months into it, I realized it wasn't for me. Luckily, I had a couple of good clients who kept me producing the amount of production I needed to keep the company happy. So I'd take care of them maybe 20 percent of the time. The other 80 percent of the time I was looking for other jobs. I used to go to the Board of Trade and spend a lot of time on the floor there. I guess I was sort of a Board of Trade groupie, but I could afford to leave the office 'cause I was able to produce what I needed. I just kept telling them I was going out on sales calls.

"After eight months, I had definitely made the decision that I was gonna come down here. It was a question of being able to get a foot in the door. All I wanted was a foot in the door—a way to get on the floor—and then you can start knocking around at other desks. After one or two things fell through, a guy I went to college with at John Carroll, got me a job as a runner in the grain room where he worked. I let them know if an opening came up in the bond room to let me know. I wanted to be in the financials because I thought that's where there would be a lot of growth and that was my interest.

"So I think I ran in the grains for three weeks. And then they did bring me over to bonds. And then I was just in a real fortunate position—the right place at the right time. The man who brought me in left to go do arbitrage upstairs, another guy left the desk two months later to work in the back office, a third guy left to go trade at the MidAm, and I immediately got thrown on the phones after only a month.

"Four months later I was running the bond desk because everyone else had left to go elsewhere. But it wasn't a problem. Since I had come from Merrill Lynch, I already understood the markets and I was used to bulls——— with people about stocks, so at least I could comfortably talk to the customers. I only needed to get down the proper procedures and what-not.

"It was an easy transition from Merrill Lynch to the Board because, well, I didn't make a lot of money at either place. You weren't on commissions when you started. So I wasn't really giving up that much when I came down here. And fortunately, I was living at home.

"Had I started with a Shearson or another big firm, I wouldn't have advanced as quickly as I did with my small firm. There, it was like, 'Hey, we're short-handed. Take this phone.' The smaller companies don't have a lot of resources to draw on when they're short people, whereas if Shearson's short they can just call somebody up from the grain room. They've got plenty of extras to call on. I mean, at Shearson, they have a training program for runners that's nine months long! Plus, there's a pecking order for runners, like runner third class and head runner. From head runner, you move up to check the orders to make sure they're properly endorsed. It's a typical large-structured company—it's very slow moving.

"Sure there are some advantages. If someone wants a structured atmosphere, then it's probably better to go into a larger company. There are also more positions in a large company, especially in, say, something like research. Maybe if you want to get into management and back office, it might be better to work for a larger firm, too, but if you want to be a trader, a floor broker, or an account executive, I'd say work for a small firm for experience. Then, I think, you have to go with a well-capitalized firm as a salesman.

"At first, I couldn't believe all the money passing hands. I remember some trader would have a $2,000 outtrade and I'd cringe inside. I remember one time when a big broker had a $300,000 outtrade. I thought the guy was gonna kill himself.

"You see guys—mostly brokers, but I won't mention any

names—who probably would have trouble counting up to
ten if you asked them and probably never got out of high
school and they're making $2,000 a day filling orders. It gave
me an incentive. I thought, 'S———, if these guys can do it, I
can, too.' But traders were different. I mean, I had jealousy
towards some of the brokers, but the traders earn it every day.
I never had anything but respect for them. But brokers? Well,
they talk about taking on a lot of risk, but I've never seen a
floor broker bust out from an outtrade. But I've seen floor
traders bust out because they lost everything.

"Like most guys, I wanted to make a quick killing, so I
made a deal with the owner of the company that I would fin-
ish out the year running the bond desk, and he was gonna
give me a seat to lease free. I'd just have to come up with the
capital.

"But in June that year, 1982, an executive approached me
from Conti and kept asking me if I wanted to come work at
Conti Commodities. I kept putting him off, saying, 'No, I
made a deal where I am and I start trading at the beginning
of the year.' So he said fine, but finally on his third approach,
he said that at least we should sit down and talk. So we did.
And he started throwing some numbers at me and said, 'You
know, there's other ways of making money in this business
besides being a trader or floor broker. You can be a
salesman—an institutional salesman and sell from the
floor.' A salesman basically talks to clients from the floor,
tells them what he perceives as happening in the markets.
A lot of the customers don't even care about your opinion
of the market, but you tell them basically what you see happening and try to get their futures trade. Anyway, after he
threw the numbers at me, I thought, well, I had nothing to
lose because, if this didn't work out, I could always try the
pits next and this would give me a lot more to walk into the
pits with, if I at least tried it.

"The executive got my name from a client he was trying to
land who said he was talking to me over at my old firm and

that he really didn't need or want the change. That's how I ended up getting recommended for the job. I can name at least five people who either left the Board of Trade or left one firm to go to another because of clients who they were talking to. In the clients' mind, talking to that person gave them the edge and, maybe, meant making a lot more money for them.

"I worked for Conti until the takeover on Sept. 6, 1984, when Refco bought it out. Refco offered us a somewhat different deal. Before the takeover, it was the typical deal. If you brought in $10 worth of trades, you'd get $2. It was 20 percent pay-out—well, 22 percent actually. Refco was a different deal. We're almost an independent company now. They charge us a flat fee to clear our trades, and anything we can get above and beyond that is kept for ourselves. We also pay all our own expenses.

"A lot of the business is relationship, and a lot of the people are very loyal to the people they talk to on the phones. Today, for example, I traded 2,000 contracts for a guy. That's equal to $100 million worth of bonds. And he depends on what I tell him. It took me two and a half years to build his trust. If somebody else comes to him and says, 'I'll do your business for $2 less per contract,' he's gonna say 'S---, it's not worth it.' The service might not be as good. Besides, a lot of my people use us not only because we execute their orders well but also because we're a clearing house of information. When one client of ours gets information, then boom, we punch all the buttons and tell all our other clients. And they like to hear it, if it's news.

"I wanted to be a trader for a long time, but now absolutely not. If things continue as they are going now, then unless you're a superb trader, the extra money that you might make in one year isn't worth the risk of having a really bad year. My average earnings over the next five years will probably be the same as the average earnings of a good trader—not a hot shot's income, but as good as 90 percent of the people in the pits. I know one guy who does the same thing I do, except he clears his trades through Shatkin, makes over a million dollars a year—easy.

"It's funny, but I'm still doing pretty much what I was doing as a phone clerk when I first started. I think the big difference—the only difference—between a phone clerk and a floor account executive is what they get paid. Sure, some clerks just write down orders like a machine—buy 100, sell 100—and that's all they do. But a lot of clerks, like my-self, established good relationships with the customers, gave them market comments, and told them what we perceived was happening on the floor that day. In that case, there's no difference between being a simple phone clerk and an ac-count executive.

"Usually, those phone clerks who do provide services that a salesman does find themselves gravitating toward a sales job and making a lot more money. They'll have a client who likes talking, and the phone clerk may decide that he thinks he can walk with this guy and go over to Shatkin or Refco and bring this guy with him and earn four times the money that he was being paid as a phone clerk. That happens quite a bit.

"Personally, I think starting as a runner is better than being a broker's assistant. If you're a broker's assistant, you're eliminating becoming a salesman from the floor. If you're a broker's assistant, you're going to be much more pit oriented. I'm not saying that a broker's assistant isn't a good job, but you're definitely eliminating certain options. Of course, if you're sure you don't want to be an AE and you definitely want to go into the pit, then that would be the way to go. If you get in with a good floor broker, then he'll set you up and sponsor you. That's a good way to go, too.

"There are a lot of other options down here other than going into the pit. There are plenty of people in financial in-stitutions all over the country—really the world—who will have to use options and futures in the future but still don't know how to use them. I feel comfortable that even if all my business dried up and I didn't want to go into the pit and trade, I could contact plenty of financial institutions and tell them that I've worked on the Chicago exchange for four years and I'd be very hirable. Even if you only work on the exchange for a year or two, you gain a lot of firsthand knowledge that you can then use to market yourself all over the country—wherever there is a financial institution that is using or should be using futures. I was in an international bank yesterday afternoon, and I ran into a guy who used to work for Delsher on the floor. Another guy I know is now with Bank of America in San Francisco. So even if you work on the floor for just a year and get to know the business, and then decide that Chicago is too cold and you want to go to California, you're marketable.

"The future growth in this industry is remarkable. We've probably only seen about 20 percent of the eventual growth. I think there's just hundreds and hundreds of S & L's that haven't even touched futures yet. Banks, too. The more innovative these S & L's and banks become the more they will be forced to go into the futures to protect themselves. But there's definitely huge growth potential.

"Someone told me when I started down here that cream rises to the top—that if you go down there and you're any good, you're going to do alright. Well, I think that's true."

## *Elizabeth*

"I started getting exposed to the markets in 1979 when I was a commodities writer for a major wire service. I wrote a daily market column that was carried in a Washington paper, a New York paper, and *The Los Angeles Times*. So I was down here every day talking to traders about how the markets were working and what was influencing them. In '79, they had the big silver crash, and I was writing stories about the Hunts and the downfall of the silver market. Well, being exposed to the markets on a daily basis sort of intrigued me, and I was hoping that in the future I would be able to get involved in this business, but I didn't realize at the time that I could lease a seat. I thought I would have to own a seat, and so the idea was pushed to the back of my mind as not being realistic at the time. But I then learned that they were leasing seats—I guess they started leasing in '78 or '79—and realized that was my opportunity to come down here."

*Elizabeth, thirty-one, began trading treasury bond futures at the Chicago Board of Trade (CBOT) in 1980. She knew nobody in the business. Although she grew up in Chicago, she didn't know about the CBOT until after she graduated from Northwestern University with a journalism degree and began writing for a major wire service. Today, she earns a six-figure income. She's one of the most successful woman traders at any exchange.*

"So I talked about it with my husband. I told him I really thought it would be something worthwhile for me to try. I said I thought that in the long term if I wanted to have a family, this would be a business that I could work mornings or afternoons or just three days a week and not have to give it up entirely. Of course, the short term opportunities to make quite a bit of money and be my own boss sounded good to me, too. So my husband said, 'Well, we've got $20,000 in the bank. Do you think that's enough to give it a shot for six months?' I said I thought so, and he said, 'O.K. I'll pay the bills while you go and try it.'

"It was very difficult for the first four months. I didn't know anybody in the pit. I was in the hole for the first four months—not much, maybe $4,000. I sort of latched on to a guy standing near me who was also relatively new, and we sort of helped each other out. He was basically my mentor. He showed me the ropes. He was only down here six months longer than I was, but he had a lot of know-how. He took me under his wing, and I learned how to trade. And the first year I did pretty well. I made about $80,000, which *I* thought was fantastic. It was close to but not quite four times what I was making as a reporter. I said, 'Oh boy, this is terrific!'

"I never thought when I came down here, 'Gee, I wonder if it's going to be harder for me because I'm a woman.' I looked at myself and thought, I wonder if I can do it. I didn't think of other people affecting my success. I thought it was up to me. And maybe that's a good attitude because I never worried about whether I was getting trades because I was a woman or whether I wasn't getting them because I was a woman. I just believed that it was my own ability that would allow me to sink or swim.

"I was one of the newer woman here. But I never found and never thought that the people in the pit discriminated against me because I was a woman. I never felt that way. If a woman wants to step out and take risks just like the men and if someone thinks they can profit from you, a hundred people will line up and make the trade with you.

"I felt that the limitations in being a woman were, number one, that your voice did not carry as well as a man's, and two, that your physical height and stature were not as helpful. If you're six feet tall and about 220 pounds, you're at a tremendous advantage here. I woudn't want to be a woman that size, but in this business it would help.

"My voice, which is not very high, has basically been ruined by shouting. But some of the other woman who have higher pitched voices do have a tremendous advantage. They are very easily heard in the pit. I guess since my voice is lower, I say it's a disadvantage to be a woman, but some woman have excellent pit voices—a real asset here. I have adapted myself to using my hands more—gesturing more—to save my voice.

"I never ran or trade checked. I wouldn't say that running and trade checking isn't important. If you don't have the money and you have a burning desire to do it, one way is to get in with a firm or get in with a broker or someone like that to learn the ropes and possibly get their spin-off, small-order decks. I'm sure that it's helpful in understanding how the markets work, too.

"But, of course, running isn't anything like trading. Deciding to enter the pits depends on whether you have the money for it. Do you have the venture capital? Do you have someone you know willing to capitalize you? I see no reason to become a runner or a broker's assistant if you've got the money. The only way you learn to trade is by doing it. You can stand outside the pit, you can trade on paper, and do everything that people do to prepare themselves, but until you're in the pit and your money is on the line, you can't really know.

"As a reporter, I learned how the markets worked but mainly from a fundamental viewpoint. In other words, the things I was looking for as a reporter were 'What has affected the market?' Was it the strike at the silver mines in the United States which caused a rise in prices? What was the actual supply and demand factor? That's what the public understands. They don't understand technical charting and things like 'the market's full of shorts and now it's going to rally.' The public understands that there was a default at a major bank and that currency prices fell, or there's an oil glut and the price of the dollar is down.

"One thing about people who are short and physically

inferior—both men and women—is that they have to be extremely aggressive. I wouldn't say that the successful women traders are smarter than the men, but I would say that they are extremely aggressive. I think that that's one of the differences I see in some of the other women who have come down here after me. They are not super aggressive. In this business, no one gives you anything. I mean, you work for every trade. Nobody taps you on the shoulder and says, 'I'll buy five.' You have to really attack the market. I'm a very aggressive trader, but I've been aggressive all my life. It's not something that I've learned down here. And you have to be fast, too. You have to see something and react. Can you learn to be fast? Well, it's difficult to learn that. But if you're not fast, you have to be smart. Luckily, I'm fast.

"One of the philosophies I had coming down here, and one that I still maintain, is that I feel that if I put my mind to something I can do almost anything that I want to do, without, of course, having to have certain physical requirements. I think that basically almost anything can be learned, and that includes trading. The will to succeed is probably 75 percent of the battle. I feel that if you want something enough, you'll do anything you have to do to be exposed to it and to succeed at it.

"I think that you have to be a little hungry to be successful down here. It has to be imperative that you make it or else you won't. That's why people who are fortunate enough not to be pressed to make a living here may not be as successful as others. You have to look at the motivations of why people are down here. I'm down here to make a living. If I left here, I'd have to go get a job because I don't have a trust fund or any wealth behind me. But some other people are not in that situation. Some come from wealthy families. They may come down here and want to meet expenses and make a little profit, but they don't feel the pressure to make money. With some of the men and women, you see people who are sort of wasting their time down here. Since you're looking at such a small group of women, it's easy to isolate them. There's only maybe a dozen women in the bond pit out of at least 400 traders. The women are such a small subculture that it's very easy to look at them and say, 'Oh Jeez, this one doesn't do anything, and this one doesn't know how to trade.' But with 400 men, it's not that easy to say, 'This one doesn't do anything.'

"I think that it's very important if you are a woman trader to try to maintain the respect that men naturally have for women. By that, I mean you try not to swear and cuss with the best of them. You try to maintain a certain amount of respect for yourself and for your peers. When I was new down here, I made a mistake bidding and offering, and one of the big traders jumped all over me and called me a foul word. I was extremely upset by that because I don't like to be talked to like that. So I mustered up my courage after the close to confront him, and I said, 'I feel you were rude to speak to me like that. I grant you I made the mistake. I was wrong. But I don't feel it's necessary to call me names. I don't call names to anybody in the pit. I don't swear at them. And I really don't appreciate being sworn at.' And the guy apologized. He's been a real nice guy, and I trade with him often. No hard feelings.

"You have to stand up for yourself whether you're man, woman, or animal. That doesn't mean throwing temper tantrums and shouting and carrying on. It just means having a little professionalism and treating the person next to you with the same respect you want to be treated with. Being a woman, I don't want people falling on top of me and pushing me and shoving me just like I'm one of the guys. Women just can't compete like that. We're not built the same way. It's nice for the guys to know that 'Hey, this is a woman—a lady— standing next to me. I'm not going to be elbowing her.' And to maintain that respect, you have to be ladylike.

"I'll tell you one way to get some perspective on this business is to have worked in another field and to know what it's like to make $10-15-20,000 a year. It gives you some perspective. You realize this is a good business and that it's worth staying in it and working at it to be successful. Sometimes when people come down here right out of college and have never really worked on a job, it comes too easy to them, and they blow it.

"To be honest, I wish I would have come down maybe a year and a half or a year sooner. When I came down, the markets were tremendously active, but I was new and trading my 1 and 2 lots for six months at a time when the markets were making some tremendous moves. But there's still a lot of opportunities. You don't have the tumultuous price movements that we had back in the late 70's and early 80's, but there's still opportunity. Incidentally, a year and a half after I was here, my husband decided that he wanted to try it. He was a funeral director in a family business. So the roles were reversed: this time I paid the bills while he came down and learned. He's been down here three years now."

# *Mike*

"I majored in accounting, but I didn't want to go into accounting because, well, accounting's kind of boring—it's not exciting. Since I didn't want to be an accountant, I figured I'd try being at the Board and see what it's like."

*Mike, twenty-three, trades bond options at the Chicago Board of Trade (CBOT) for Singer-Wenger. Singer-Wenger is one of several firms at the CBOT that hires traders to trade for them. It provides its traders with a membership, instruction in trading strategy, a base salary between $15,000 and $30,000 a year, plus a percentage of the firm's total profits. The trader's personal financial risk is zero. As Mike told me, "If I lose money, I'll lose my job. That's it. They'll say, 'You're through, you're a lousy trader,' and they'll fire me." He started with the firm after graduating from the University of Wisconsin in December 1983. After working as a clerk for six months, he began trading in June 1984. Out of college for less than one and a half years, at the time he was interviewed Mike was earning between $50,000–$60,000 a year.*

"Singer-Wenger backs me financially. It's their money that I'm trading. I'm a salaried broker for them. It's their own membership. I don't have to pay a thing. I'm just the managerial nominee. It's the company's seat transferred to my name. And I trade their money. They give me verbal orders to execute in the morning, and I execute them all day. I get a salary and a commission at the end of the year based on how well the company has done. In the pit, I have total discretion. The verbal orders they give me are general directions—do this, do that—but I have discretion as to when I do them. In other words, they may say buy these calls at a certain volatility. Well, I decide when to buy them—I decide even when those calls are trading at that volatility because it's not too easy to figure out. You can't just say, 'Well, now they're trading at that particular volatility. I better buy them.' It's more complicated than that. You have to decide if they really are at a particular volatility or not. It's not like you have a computer with you in the pit.

"They take all the risk. And you can be sure that if I made $300,000 one year, then there was the risk that I could have lost $600,000. They assume all the risk, so it's not that much of a bummer when I see myself making, maybe, $100,000 for the company and earning half that as my income.

"If I make $300,000 and other people for the company lose money, then there's not going to be that much money to be distributed because we pool it all together. So if I make $300,000 and another guy loses $300,000, then neither of us are going to get anything. That's the bad deal about it. Supposedly, we're all good traders. They dump the bad traders and keep the good ones. The idea is we're all going to make money.

"I started with them as a clerk. They hired me to trade, but they wanted me to clerk first. You can't just throw someone in the pit. They've got to have experience. I clerked for six months. I stood at the bond pit and flashed hand signals to the options traders, which told them where the market was. I also relayed verbal orders from them to the brokers in the bond pit. I got experience through that, and after six months they thought I was ready to get in the pit. I traded small for three months, basically just scalping, getting in and out every day. After three months, I made some bucks and started putting on spreads and stuff and trading a little riskier. And that's what I've been doing ever since.

"In those first six months, I was making $200 a week. I was living at home and hardly had any expenses. But, believe me, $200 a week is barely enough to live on even without any expenses.

"Before I graduated college, I knew I wanted to be in the commodities business, so I got a job as a runner for three months in between my senior year and the extra semester

I took to graduate. It took me four and a half years to graduate from Wisconson. I worked for Refco at the Board, and during that summer, I heard about this company hiring traders, so I gave them an application. I applied to about 100 other firms, too. I knocked on every door and gave them applications and a resume. I decided on Singer-Wenger over a few other firms who offered me a job.

"Oh yeah, another reason I worked as a runner that summer was because I liked the hours—8 a.m. to 2 p.m. Can't beat that! It was the summer. I wanted to goof around, and I didn't really care about money then.

"To be honest, back then Singer-Wenger was a young company. We had five people when I started, and people were getting in the pit faster back then. Whereas O'Connor, another company that also puts people in the pit, had 300 people working for them.

"I worked as a trade checker for them for only about a month or so—both in the morning and the evening. It was part of the training process before I became a trader.

"But I personally don't think trade checking's that important. It's a real s----- way to get into the business. When you're a trader, you learn how to deal with outtrades because all outtrades are is 'Do you know this? Do you remember this trade?' 'No, I don't.' 'O.K., so I'm not going to accept it.' Or you say, 'Oh yea, I remember that; I forgot to card it. I'll accept the trade.' That's all an outtrade is. You don't have to know how to go through and delete things off the outtrade sheets and say, 'It's 2 vs. 1, but he wants 2 in his name, blah, blah, blah.' Who needs to know that? As far as I'm concerned, that's bookkeeping work. All you've got to know as a trader is if you made the trade or not. That's all it is. Why do you have to trade check to learn how to do that?

"I will agree with one thing. It's a way to earn more money. It's something about the business that you don't have to learn if you want to be a trader. If you want to run a clearing house someday, then, yea, it's a good thing to learn. But how many people plan to have their own clearing house? For me, I'd rather just trade and make a nice living and never have to deal with my own clearing house.

"The best experience you can have is being a broker's assistant or an arbitrage clerk or something like that, where you're standing around the pit and can see in the pit. I stood at the edge of the pit and reported where the market was with hand signals. You can get somewhat of a feel for things that way.

"It's a tough world down here. The way to do it is to start from the bottom, knock on doors, get a job as a runner, and use your own judgment. Running gives you the exposure. That's all you need. You don't really even need a book like this.

"People should just come down and be a runner and take it from there. You move up fast if you're good. A good runner quickly becomes a phone clerk. A good phone clerk will always find a position with another company at a higher pay. There's always positions opening up. Eventually, if you're a good phone clerk, you're going to start getting your own accounts. You're going to need a seat for that. And eventually, you'll make a lot of money and be able to go into the pit and trade on your own. It may take five or ten years, but it's the route that most people who start without any money take. Other people work for an independent trader or broker and count cards or whatever and then the trader will back you in some way. Maybe he'll say 'Here's 50 grand' and put the money in your account so you can rent a seat, and then split 50-50 whatever you make. Those are the two routes you can take to become a trader.

"Trade-link, Singer-Wenger, CRT—there's loads of firms that hire clerks. And at the Chicago Board of Options Exchange (CBOE), there's millions of rich people who hire a clerk, and if they like him, they back him and they take a 50 percent or 40 percent share of his profits. So there's plenty of ways to get backed if you're good.

"Basically, I'm a trader now because I always wanted to do something on my own. I caught a lucky break. These guys hired me, and I got in at the right time."

# *Jim*

"After I got out of school, I sold copiers for Xerox in White Plains, New York. I liked the company, but soon found out I wasn't crazy about door-to-door selling. I wasn't terrible at it, but let's just say I didn't excel at it. I knew there was something better out there. So I sat down with my dad, who was a partner in charge of running the New York operation of a Chicago brokerage company. I said, 'This job sucks. I'm sick of it. What's going on in Chicago?' He said, 'You can go to Chicago, be a runner, and see how you do.'"

*Jim, twenty-seven, a 1979 graduate of the University of Michigan, began at the Chicago Board of Trade (CBOT) in September 1980 as a clerk. He worked for a year and a half as a runner, phone clerk, and trade checker before leaving in February 1982 to trade for himself at the Mid-American Commodity Exchange (MidAm). After six months there, he returned to the CBOT as the personal floor broker for one of Goodman-Manaster's biggest customers and also to trade for himself. It was a great deal. The money he earned from the brokerage freed him from the anxiety of making money right away as a trader. He didn't have to rely on his pit trading as his sole means of income. When interviewed, he was earning roughly $80,000 a year.*

"I went to work for an account executive who drummed up his own business but cleared his trades through Goodman-Manaster. In the beginning I was his errand boy: I answered the phone and helped him out when things were busy. I tried to be as watchful and as helpful as I could. After a couple months when I earned his trust and, just as important, the trust of his clients, my job became more interesting because there was more I could do. People would ask me questions—they wanted to hear my answers. They might say, 'Buy ten bonds,' and if I wanted to work the order for a minute or so, I could. That made the job fun.

"If I were a runner for Paine-Webber or Merrill Lynch, I would have been a runner for six months to a year. And I would have been a phone clerk *only* if I got the big promotion. And even then I wouldn't have been given a fraction of the responsibility I was given at Goodman. If you're really good, it's much harder to be noticed—much harder to stand out—in a big firm. But at Goodman, the owner's hiring philosophy helped me out. He just threw s——— against the wall and kept what stuck. He hired a lot of people rather cheaply who were no good. They came and went quickly. But if you were good, you stood out and quickly became a phone clerk. And if you were good, you got to know the customers and they got to know you. If they liked you and trusted you, they'd ask you questions. And that was the part of the job I enjoyed.

"At Goodman, the big accounts were houses that had their own retail accounts, so all you're watching are a lot of small retail clients—doctors and lawyers throughout the country putting in 1 and 2 lot orders. I don't think there's anything to learn from watching them, except ... I take that back. There is a lot to learn: You're not going to be knocked over by their expertise, but you can learn a lot from their mistakes. And that's important. We had some traders who traded with their firm's accounts, and if they were doing well, they were good to watch. They all had different trading strategies. Some charted and tried to pick points to take 3 or 5 ticks. Some guys tried to catch a trend–move to take half a point or a point.

"I worked for six months. Then somebody left the bond desk to trade, and so in the summer of 1981, I went to the bond desk as a phone clerk. I worked there until February 1982, about eight months, when I began trading for myself at the MidAm.

"What's the old economics term? The law of diminishing returns. As a runner and a phone clerk, there's a lot to learn and a lot to see in the first year. And then I think the return of the time you spend becomes less and less valuable. I think it's great to be a runner for two or three months. If you're smart, after that it's a waste of time. A phone clerk is different because it's a catch-all title. It can refer to somebody who does nothing but pick up the phone and write down buy or sell, all the way to someone, like a floor account executive, who spends a lot of time just calling up people, soliciting their business, trying to give them information, and earning their trust. You know, when people call you up they don't expect you to know where the market's going, but what they do hope is that you will be able to give them information faster than someone else will.

"At Goodman, there's only so far a phone clerk can go. It's a discount brokerage house. Goodman doesn't offer the services that other houses do and it doesn't charge what other houses do. So it's good at Goodman if you don't make mistakes—you gain confidence in your own abilities, and earn the respect of the customers. The customers like to try to tap you for information to see what you've picked up from the other sources on the floor. Maybe they knock some ideas off you. Or maybe they just like talking to you. If you're a good bulls————that's a good tool to have.

"At other houses, the customers may be a little more, say, scientific, or at least their trading strategies may be a little more advanced. They're looking for, maybe, computer assistance, or maybe they're just more involved in options trading. The more the customers know, if you're smart, the more you'll learn from them.

"That's where you're limited working for a small company, like Goodman, rather than a larger firm. Big companies have more dimensions. They're likely to have a lot more people in the company to learn from, and you can make more opportunities in a company like that. But I think a smaller company is a much better springboard. If you're smart and can make opportunities happen, you can do a hell of a lot more in a smaller company in the first year or two than, I think, you can at a company like Drexel. On the other hand, if you come out of Harvard with an MBA or something, you'd probably do better going into a larger company in their finance department or something.

"The runners who are runners for a few years are probably runners because they're too stupid to do anything else and haven't proven themselves capable of advancing. Runners that are good soon become phone clerks. No matter how big a company is they're not going to let someone who is intelligent and capable be a runner for a year or two. It's a waste of their time, and they fear that if you're competent and you know you are, you're not going to remain a runner some place for a year or two.

"I checked trades in the afternoons from September 1980 until September 1982. I never checked trades in the morning because the hours overlapped with my job as a clerk at the bond desk. You could check trades in the morning and be a phone clerk at the grain desk because their markets open an hour and a half later than the bonds.

"If you want to be a trader, I think trade checking is important. It's a different facet of the business. It directly affects you when you're trading. You're going to have outtrades. And you leave yourself open—people can take advantage of you—if you don't understand the workings of outtrades. You've got to know it—it's probably going to cost you money. If you know what happens, sometimes it makes it easier to retrace those trades that are out and, possibly, find that the trade checkers made a mistake, and discover that it's not you that's out, but another trader. That's happened to me, and I've saved myself a little money. You know, there's so much money on the line, it's silly not to understand exactly what's going on.

"But there again, the law of diminishing returns takes over quickly. It doesn't take long to know how outtrades work. For someone who wants to be a trader, there's no reason to spend every afternoon for years and years checking trades. I did it for two years because I needed the money, which was about $100 extra a week, but that was more than enough.

"I made $12,000 a year when I first started working as a clerk during the day and a checker at night. I was working twelve hours a day. I got a raise after six months, but let me tell you, I didn't come close to becoming rich. You can't save much money working as a clerk. You can, though, make a lot of money as a morning trade checker—as much as $50,000 a year. If you're good and check trades for a lot of traders, and they do well, they're usually pretty nice to you around Christmas. My first Christmas at the Board was pretty surprising. I've never seen so much money and so many gifts flying around. That's an accepted way of doing business that I had never been exposed to before.

"If you're in commodities and you see all the money that's made and lost, you get kind of warped. You think that people are playing monopoly, except that it's real money. You know, when I graduated college, I thought somebody making $20,000 a year was making good money. And today, I know what I make, but if I compare it to what other people at the Board are making, I don't feel terribly successful, or even feel that I'm making a lot of money. But if I look at people I know from college who aren't in the business—well they might be doing pretty well—but if they knew what I was making, they'd think I was making a hell of a lot of money.

"The bottom line in this business is money. A trader isn't working up a corporate hierarchy. There's no profit sharing; there's no pension; there's no health benefits. You're not getting anything, except maybe a bigger bank balance. And after ten years if you haven't made any money, you've really wasted a lot of time. Not only haven't you succeeded in the business, but you haven't developed any kind of career. You have the opportunity to make a hell of a lot of money down here, but you give up a lot of security, too. It's a gamble.

"Trading? I never gave a second thought about doing it. I do not view it as a life or death situation, but it's easy for me or any person in my shoes to do it. I'm not married, I don't have any kids, I don't have any major financial commitments. I've talked to some of my twenty-six and twenty-seven-year-old friends about the business. They're making $30,000 or $40,000 a year and at this point in their lives, they couldn't drop down to $15,000 or $20,000 to be a clerk or something. They're not really willing to invest two years or so at a very low salary to make a lot more money five years down the road. It's a decision that's easy to make when you're twenty-two, but much harder to make when you get older.

"If you just start off as a runner, you're only making $125 a week. It's impossible to do that unless you're living at home or you're a street person. You can't pay your own rent or buy your own food on $125 a week. So most of the runners are younger kids. What I'm saying is that it's tough to begin a career. Now I make more money than my friends who I went to school with, but when I started off they all made more money than I did. And that's hard to take. You don't walk around feeling terribly successful.

"Before I went down there, I wasn't aware at all of the risks—how much money you could make and lose. But like almost every other youngster who goes down there, my eyes opened wide when I saw how much money people make. You say to yourself, 'Boy, I'd like to take a crack at that,' or 'I'd like to make a million dollars, too.' It's also very illusionary because if you're down there for a year or two you get to know a lot of people and it seems the same faces are in the pit day after day, year after year. If you're there, it's because you're successful. But you quickly forget the faces that are here today and gone two months down the road. And it's easy to forget all the people that have failed. But as a runner and as a clerk, you get to watch people make so many mistakes that you have to be naive or blind not to recognize that you can lose a lot of money. It's pretty easy to fail. But at twenty-four, with no wife, no kid, no responsibilities, there was no better time to take that chance.

"I started at the the MidAm because, I like to say, the tuition is cheap there. The contracts are half the size as the Board's or the Merc's. So if you screw up, it'll only cost you half as much. If you lose a tick on a 1 lot, it'll cost you approximately $15 at the MidAm and $30 at the Board of Trade. Also, the caliber of traders at the MidAm is not nearly as good as that at the Board of Trade. So it's easier to break in. You don't have to be as fast. At the Board of Trade, if you're not on the ball, there are 100 other guys that will make the trade before you. At the MidAm, you've got a lot of guys who are lost, who don't have a lot of money, whose hands shake a lot more, and who don't have the staying power financially. It's competitive, but the level of skill isn't there. I was there six months before I went to the Board of Trade. At the MidAm, there's very little paper. So if you trade actively, you're trading with locals and trying to pick each other's pocket. And not everybody can make money. The good ones do and the bad ones go back to being salesmen.

"I wasn't real successful at the MidAm. My biggest problem when I first started trading was that I didn't have very much money, and I didn't like to lose what I had. You can't make money in the business unless you're willing to take a risk. As I slowly made money and slowly could risk more, I was more successful. But I found that to be a much longer process for me than it was for some other people.

"I got to know the guy I work for now as a broker pretty well when I was a phone clerk. He was a customer of Goodman's—the kind of customer that made the job interesting for me. I developed a good rapport with him. He wasn't the type of person who asked me whether I thought the market was going up or down. He made his own decisions. But he would give me a little discretion on orders. Maybe he would say "Buy 20," so I got to decide whether I wanted to pay 6 for them or try to get 5 or maybe 4. And that made the job a lot of fun. You felt as if someone trusted you. You felt a little more important than someone who just picked up the phone and wrote buy 10 or sell 10 at the market.

"So he hired me as his personal broker at the Board of Trade, which meant I was at his beck and call, but when I didn't have an order to fill for him, I could trade for myself. The company owned a seat and transferred it to my name. They provided me with a seat but I was at their beck and call. The bad part was that if I was trading and they wanted an order filled, I had to drop everything. The good part was that I had a seat available, and I had half of my time free to do whatever I wanted. Also, I started at a small salary, so I had something coming in. I didn't have to worry about money to buy food or pay the rent. I had enough to cover all my bills. And that was nice for me because I'm not such a crap shooter that I can just walk into the pit and assume a lot of risk—risk way out of proportion to the amount of money I have. I had to build slowly, taking more risk as I became more successful.

"Nepotism is probably underrated at the Board of Trade. I know very few people who are down here who didn't have a relative in the business. I wouldn't be in the business if my father wasn't in it. As I look around at the people I know at the Board of Trade, I'd say 95 percent of them are there directly because they had a relative in the business or a very close acquaintance. I think it's a tough business to get into if you just walk off the street not knowing anybody—you know, if you just walk around and pass out your resume. Everybody down there is down there because they had a father or a brother down there. You don't have to have a father in the business, but it helps. It helps in any business. But it's not a requirement.

"There are some jobs that you're not going to get unless you have the right father. To take the extreme, you're not going to become a specialist at the stock exchange unless your grandfather was. But there are plenty of other opportunities, if somebody's good and personable and makes the right connections. You know, there's as much politics down here as there is anywhere.

"But when you wake up in the morning, if you don't want to go to work, you don't have to. You can go to the track, play golf, or anything. Even I have a lot more leeway than all my friends from college who are not in commodities. I still owe a lot of allegiance to my boss, but now three quarters of my day is spent doing my own thing. I have the luxury to go on vacation whenever I want; I can leave early if I want. By no means, do I have the responsibility that you have at IBM or Xerox where you're in a corporate hierarchy. I think the best of all worlds is being a successful local. You're your own boss, which is what most people in the world want to be."

# *Scott*

"I worked down at the options exchange during the summer between my sophomore and junior year at Wesleyan and saw that you could make money. There were guys there year after year who made money consistently. I'd always heard about the guys who made millions and then lost millions, but what impressed me were the guys who made a steady income day in and day out. So in the back of my mind, I always knew there was a Board of Trade that I could go to. And I decided, if worse came to worse after I graduated, I could always make a living that way."

*Scott, twenty-five, graduated from Wesleyan University in 1981, majoring in English. He began as a runner at the Chicago Board of Options Exchange (CBOE) in August 1981 for Shearson, where he worked for three months. He then worked for a year as a clerk for First Boston Co. at the Chicago Board of Trade (CBOT), followed by a stint as a phone clerk for an arbitrage operation for three months. After that he was an assistant to an independent trader, again at the Options Exchange, for three months. In between his various jobs, he has spent ten months on unemployment compensation. In November 1983, he began trading bond options at the CBOT. In his first year and a half of trading, he has earned approximately $30,000.*

"After I graduated in 1981, I came back to Chicago knowing I'd get a job somewhere. I walked around the stock options exchange, and I stopped at every single firm and said I had experience and would like a job as a runner. I knew that it wouldn't be very difficult and that within a month's time—no problem—I'd find a job at a very high-paying $170 a week. (Laugh) I had eight weeks experience on the options exchange, so that would help me. Plus, I was a college graduate.

"I started at Shearson. They knew I wasn't going to go and

smoke too much reefer during lunch. They figured that I knew where the different stocks were, which was important. At this time there was active trading in a lot of different stocks, and runners were important because time was essential. Your order could get lost by a runner trying to find where the stock option was located. And if it did, it would arrive fifteen minutes late and a hell of a lot of money later, too.

"I lasted three months there. My promotion—believe it or not—would have been from a runner to a paper shredder, meaning you tear the teletype orders that come off the machine. The next step is you get to take some of the phone orders and give them to the runners. It was ridiculous. There were fifty runners and ten paper shredders at max, and then when things were slow, they'd have thirty runners. They'd come and go. They're such small chips for the firm. A runner? Twelve thousand a year.

"I was then lucky to get a job with First Boston, which was just starting up operations at the options. They were going to trade Ginnie Mae options, which never went through. The girl I worked for—and it's interesting I worked for a girl because there are not that many woman on the floor, and the ones that are on the floor have to be better than a man— worked for a while with another woman who asked me if I wanted to work for First Boston. She knew me through the grapevine. She knew I was trying to get somewhere, that I had a head on my shoulders, and was a college graduate.

"I started as the head 'go-fer'—the only go-fer—since there was only her and another guy in the operation with me. They asked me what I wanted for my salary. At the time, the highest paid runners on the floor of the options exchange were making $1,000 a month. I told them that, considering what they were asking me to do—be extremely flexible, be a trainee, and a go-fer—I'd say my salary requirements were between $1,000 and $1,500 a month. They came in right in the middle at $1,250, which I figured they would. But it made me the highest paid runner on the floor. I was making $15,000 a year, which is a lot for a runner, considering you get off at 2:00. Anyway, the Ginnie Mae options never went through at the options exchange, so First Boston decided to trade Ginnie Mae futures at the Board of Trade. I began working there.

"The first three months were spent up in the office, just learning about the business. After that I was a runner on the floor and then I became a phone clerk. I also checked trades in the morning. I wasn't the trade checker, but sometimes the guy slept late and this and that. I helped out in the afternoon, too. Basically, I learned how to do everything, but I wasn't anything. I should have worn a sign, 'Main Go-fer'."

"And then after a year, I missed out on their bonus, and somebody offered me a job doing arbitrage between the notes and the bonds. We were mostly trading the notes against the bonds, but occasionally we would trade cash against futures. I started that in January '84, and it lasted about three months. Then I was fired, well, let go. I lost $1,500 total over those three months, which, I thought, was really negligible. I was dealing with brokers who were incompetent. We would always get picked-off and we were giving up 1 tick on both sides, which is too much. So, honestly, I thought it was good being down only $1,500 after learning how to trade for the first time. True, I wasn't great. I wasn't a natural or anything, but I could keep afloat. I learned that at least. But they decided to cut the line, and I was out.

"Next, I collected unemployment for about three months, maybe four months, which pays pretty well when your salary was eighteen grand a year. That's what I had been making—plus bonus. Unemployment came out to $700 cash a month—unbelievable. That's more than some runners clear in a month. You can live all right on that, especially because I had saved $1,000 for the summer. So I had $1,000 cash per month for four months. I had a good time and went to a lot of Cubs' games.

"At the same time, I wrote a lot of letters and talked to a lot of people and finally got a job back at the options exchange with a man who owns a huge local clearing house at the CBOE. He had about a half a million dollar portfolio, and I worked for him about three months. We traded the OEX, IBM, Honeywell, and Hewlett-Packard. Basically, he would put big spreads on, and I would have to adjust them. I'd also get to decide when to cover certain positions. It wasn't my money, but it was a great experience. He paid me $1,000 a month and then gave me a $1,000 bonus. He told me, 'If you stop biting your nails, I'll give you $1,000.' So I did.

"And then he let me go. After three months, he said he's not gonna do it anymore. He had paid me $4,000; but he made over $100,000. But what did he care? The man has several houses, and he's got half a million dollars in his trading account. And he didn't want some kid to handle it while he was on vacation. He didn't want to worry about it. So he fired me. What did he care?

"And then I collected unemployment for another six months until a friend gave me $10,000 to trade with. This friend knew me since seventh grade. We weren't real close, but he knew me that long. That means something. So he gave me ten grand to trade with, and I started trading bond options in November 1983.

"The stipulations were pretty easy to explain. We wrote up a contract that was about a paragraph long—maybe three sentences—both signed it, and shook hands. It said: 'Here's $10,000. We split the profits 50-50. After the first $50,000, I get 60 percent of the profits. This agreement is good until either there's less than $2,000 in the account or I buy him out.' I could buy him out at any time.

"He was a trader himself. He traded Polaroid stock options and had done very well. He was happy to give me a chance and to make a little bit of money off it, too.

"I learned a lot by observing him. He gave me great advice

in terms of temperament. He would make a lot of money but not take on a lot of risk. He always hedged himself and was very disciplined. I learned from his trading more than from his directly telling me anything about strategy.

"I bought him out after eight months. He wasn't too happy about it 'cuz he was taking the big risk—ten grand. But he made about five grand on the deal, which in less than a year is 60 percent return. He couldn't really complain financially. He came out alright.

"He got a little uptight when things got bad, but that's also when he was at his best. When I said, 'I didn't do so good this week,' he'd encourage me and when I got it back, he'd call it a victory. Of course, when you're just starting off you're just trying to keep afloat. He was always morally supportive.

"He also helped me lease the membership at a discount of $100 a month. I was able to lease a seat for $150 a month from the firm where my backer started. The going rate was about $250.

"I paid all my debts and now have twenty grand to my name. When you come to think of it, that's great. I just started. I'm my own boss. I take off when I want. Of course, it's also hard being so directly in control of your own fate.

"In my pit, almost all the people I know have been there from the time I started. I'm one of the few new faces that has remained. Since I've been there—a year and a half now—I haven't noticed very many new faces. What I mean is, I've noticed a lot of new faces but they all seem to come and go. Not many have stayed like I have. I've seen more than ten people come and go since I've been here. A friend of mine says this place is like a revolving door.

"I'd say my year at First Boston was very valuable in that I learned different angles that you wouldn't learn on the floor. I learned how the retail business works, and I learned who the outside customers were, and I learned how an investment bank works. But if you're asking me did it help my trading once I was on my own? Well, I can't say. You know, they say trading is something that can't be taught but can be learned. So on that basis, you can't say, 'Go do this or go do that, and it'll teach you how to be a good trader.' Different experiences helped me to be more knowledgeable. I could see how the traders off the floor traded. It helped me learn some market psychology—how the outside traders think and what factors they consider. It gave me confidence that I wasn't out of touch with the outside. I'm not unfamiliar with it or intimidated by it.

"You know, when you're standing in the pit and, my God, Merrill Lynch or Hutton comes at you with hundreds after hundreds after hundreds, you panic and say, 'Well, what the hell do they know?' Well, they do know something. There's always a reason why they're buying the stuff. They may have better, more recent information. Their size can be intimidating as hell, especially to a guy like me who's standing in the pit just trying to make a little bit on each trade. They'll just blow you right out of there.

"There are a lot of guys down here who don't know anything. They read the *Sun-Times* sports section, and that's it. They don't even read the business section. A *Wall Street Journal* has never even graced their hands. They don't know where to find the credit markets in the back section. And they do fine. Some of them make more money than I can even imagine. But other people like me care a little more about what the outside world is thinking—maybe because I hope to be on the outside sometime. Maybe I'll call in my orders from the yacht. Now that's not too bad, huh?

"I'm the exception down here. Most people really like it here. I don't like it like they do. It's not a passion for me on a day to day basis. Some of them can't do without the excitement and intensity. When they're away, they miss the action too much. They have to go back to it.

"My main feeling is that this is the hardest place to make easy money. That's an old saying, but it's true. You can make a lot of money in a very short time here. It can be done. There's a lot of intensity and a lot of concentration and a lot of wear and tear, but you can make it fast—faster than anywhere else, I think.

"I was a gopher for a couple of years, traded slowly for a couple years, and I hope the next couple will bring home the gravy. But I really don't want to stay down here for more than five years. If I make $5 million by the time I'm thirty or if I save $50,000 or even if I make just a good living for every year I'm down here but spend most of it and have just a little bit to show for it, I still want to be out of here.

"Right now, if I were to put away 100 grand, which is not totally unrealistic 'cuz I just put away $20,000 in a year and a half—my first year and a half—of trading, I would leave. I'd leave here and go up to some place near a school, like Madison, or possibly some place out west, and read and write.

"I'd hope I'd accomplish something with my writing—I'd give myself a couple of years to do that. And then I could always come back here if I wanted to. But I just can't see doing this straight for a long time."

# Gary

"In late-1979-early-1980, I was looking to change careers. I was fooling around from the outside in commodities. The metals growth was just about petering out. The New York Futures Exchange (NYFE) was just getting ready to open. I went to a few of the NYFE seminars—real dog and pony shows. I was thinking of buying a NYFE seat to trade currencies. But I wanted to work as a runner for a month to see how the NYFE took off. I didn't want to shell out any money for something before it proved itself. Besides, it all sounded too good to be true. You've got to be suspicious of anybody who shows you a nice, neat marketing plan, like the NYFE did, of how they're going to have 10 percent of the commodity business after only one year and the value of the seats are sure to double. So I went down and worked for a clearing house as a runner for $150 a week. And I knew after two days that the currencies weren't going to make it. The floor was beautiful: they had every kind of equipment you could imagine— comtrends, Reuters, quotation screens—everywhere. There were clerks everywhere—no booth was empty. The only problem was that the phones never rang, and there were five traders in the pits. The bonds traded for about six months, but the NYFE didn't have a chance to begin with. I realized that I couldn't trade down there, and it wasn't worth buying a membership."

*Gary, thirty-three, vice-president of a clearing house in New York, began as a $150 a week runner for the firm in 1980 at age twenty-seven. He has a master's in economics from the University of Arizona. He offers a sobering picture of the New York markets. While he sees tremendous opportunities there, he knows most of the stories about the pits are exaggerated. "There is not so much new blood in the pits," he says. He earns around $65,000 a year.*

"So there I was: twenty-seven, with a master's in economics, making $150 a week as a runner. It just happened at the time that another job opened up at the clearing house I'm with now as operations manager, which I got. Basically, I worked for a month and jumped from being a runner to the operations manager in New York. It wasn't that big a deal. We were a pretty small company then. We just had our New York office. There were only eight people working here. Now we have thirty-five people here. Then we were only clearing the NYFE, which meant we were doing 500 contracts a day compared to 15,000 today. There's a big difference. To make an analogy to a restaurant, it would be like managing one of those hot dog stands on the street and managing a McDonalds.

"As the company expanded, as we moved over to the COMEX and other exchanges, we started getting more business, and I moved up to assistant vice-president and then vice-president. Back in 1980, I oversaw the operations of the company. I made sure that the traders' statements were all correct, all the balancing had been done properly. Now, we have an in-house computer system, and a key-punch department. This office itself is about five times the size of our original office five years ago.

"Originally, I wanted to be a trader but not anymore. First, in New York, I don't really see the great success stories that everyone talks about. There aren't twenty-two and twenty-three-year-olds making $300,000 or $400,000 a year. Maybe in the late 70's but not today, and not in New York. At the Commodity Exchange (COMEX), where we primarily deal, the people who are making a lot of money are the ones who are entrenched there. You can't just walk into the pit and make money anymore. You really can't. The paper's not there, and just to get in now costs $100,000 in liquid assets. If you don't have that, you have to have somebody put up $100,000 for you in a T-bill, and then you have to have trading capital, too. The COMEX is a very closed exchange. The NYFE, on the other hand, is the exact opposite. But that's because trading at the NYFE is like playing class A minor league ball compared to the COMEX. Right now, the seats are going for $2,000, and you can lease a seat for $1 a year. Only a handful of people make decent money down there. Only one person last year made seven-figures. Everyone's a speculator; there's not enough liquidity to scalp. It's basically locals against arbitrageurs. Probably less than twenty traders made even six-figures at the NYFE. It's not that lucrative a market.

"I don't mean to paint a bleak picture of the New York markets—just a realistic one. The exchanges simply aren't what a lot of people think they are. People don't automatically make $100,000, $200,000, or $500,000. In New York, it's not that easy. At the COMEX, yeah, there's people who have been there for years who make a lot of money, but there's not that much new blood coming in that makes it. I'm only saying that getting to the big time in New York is a real struggle.

"In this business, it used to be that people got into it through the family—third generation deals. Most of the people, at least on the New York end, were not college graduates. They were mostly high school drop-outs. They came down here at sixteen or eighteen and went to work. They worked as runners and clerks for a while and worked their way up. The whole NY commodities industry was a very closed and isolated world.

"But in the last five years all this has changed. People have started looking at the business from more sophisticated angles. The industry has broadened its scope. It's moved into cash settlement contracts; there's more arbitrage opportunities; there's equity options and now non-equity options. Before that, it was a pretty straightforward business. Basically, all you had to know was who the other traders were in the pit, make friends with them, and, if you got in with them, you'd probably make money. Five years ago, you didn't see a guy coming down on the floor with an MBA. Three years ago, I remember somebody left the COMEX floor to get an MBA at Harvard, and people were laughing at him. The industry is getting to the point where education is becoming more and more important.

"The reason? A lot of the opportunities in this business are moving away from the floor. The guys today who come in with MBA's aren't really going to the floor. They're going upstairs and trading for firms and doing arbitrage between options and futures. Five years ago, things were different—not nearly so sophisticated. You could go down to the COMEX and guys made money by buying in the morning and selling in the afternoon, or just standing near a broker who was their friend.

"If you're coming out of school with an MBA from Northwestern or Columbia in finance with a specialization in commodities, you can do anything you want in the field. You can get a job with Salomon Bros. But if you're coming out of Oshkosh U. with a liberal arts degree or if you're coming out of high school and don't want to go to college, going to the floor is the best route to move in this business, whether what you want is actually trading on the floor or finding an opportunity to trade upstairs. We've had a lot of people from here who have gone on from being phone clerks and runners at $15-20,000, and now they're upstairs trading for firms or they're running an arbitrage operation on the floor, making $25-30,000.

"I've got a guy working for us who is a high school dropout, and has ten earrings in his ear. He makes good money. He makes a lot more here than he could probably in any other job on the outside. He runs this place at night—does the computer work. He used to be a trade checker. Now if he went to another industry and walked in with his muscle t-shirt and skull tattoo on his arm, they'd say, 'Well, we don't have an opening right now. Why don't you check back with us in about forty years?' This place is a good opportunity, especially for people who don't want to go to college. A lot of guys here are only high school grads making $30,000 a year, and they're just twenty-one years old, which isn't bad. You figure that when they're twenty-three, they will have earned close to $100,000 in just three years. A college grad comes out of school in debt $30,000, and then he's got to start at the bottom, earning $18-or-20,000, assuming he doesn't come out with an accounting or engineering degree. Also, the young guys here got a chance to hook up with somebody who may sponsor them and put them into the trading pit.

"In the paper yesterday, I read that the average manufacturing raise was 6 percent. You look at that, and then you get a better feel of how this place compares. Sure, some of the people down here start off at $11,000, but after a year, they may be making $20,000, which means in one year, as a high school graduate, they've had a 75 percent raise.

"It's pretty hard these days to go from being a clerk to making $250,000 trading. You could do that five years ago. In Chicago, maybe you still can. I don't know. It's possible. But the new capital requirements make it difficult: at the Chicago Board of Trade (CBOT), you've got to have $50,000 to lease a seat now, and at the Merc, you need $25,000. They're not giving people 'shots' anymore. They've stopped saying, 'O.K., you've only got $10,000, well, we'll let you trade 1 lots.' Why? It's a much more capital intensive business now. A few years back, you could work a couple jobs, scrape together $5,000, maybe borrow $5,000, and give it a shot. Can't do it anymore. The firms can't afford the 'haircuts.' A firm must pay for every lessee it has on their books who doesn't have X dollars in his account. So if a firm clears 50 people, it can't take a $25,000 'haircut.' It'll go out of business.

"You've got to look at the situation this way. The chances for a high school kid to do anything now is very limited. So maybe you can't expect realistically to come down here and make $200,000 trading, but you've still got a good shot to make $30-40,000 before you're twenty-five as a clerk or manager, and you still have a shot to make a lot of money. It's still a business where, regardless of the fact that people are looking more towards education, if you've got a performance record, then education means nothing. In a lot of businesses, if you don't have an MBA you walk into a wall finally and can't go any farther. Here, it's different. It's a business where performance is the final judge. I hired a runner who had graduated from Wharton. He was here for about a year, but couldn't cut it. He was terrible. Another guy, who started here at the same time as he did, was his boss three months later. He had gold chains, a crew-cut, and no college.

"I get resumes all the time from MBA's. I never even bother looking at them. I'd never hire an MBA for the floor. I'm looking for someone who is hungry and realizes this is a chance that he wouldn't get anywhere else. I ask every MBA: "Do you think you could work for someone nineteen years old, who's gonna be telling you what to do and reads *The Daily News* while you read *The Wall Street Journal?"* People don't read *The Wall Street Journal* down here. Some people do. But there's a lot of traders who make a lot of money who never get past *The Daily News'* sports section.

"I usually hire people who just happen to show up at the right time when somebody is leaving. Otherwise, if I'm looking for somebody, I'll ask people I know in the industry and hire somebody that way, by word-of-mouth. You end up with a lot of insiders, but that's how the industry is. In our company, we've got three sets of brothers working for us and half the other people are friends. But if you hit the rooms where the trade checkers hang out and start asking if a company needs runners or trade checkers, sooner or later you're going to hit somebody who's quitting or moving up. You can always get into the crack if you're there at the right time."

# *Henry*

"I graduated from Southern Illinois in December 1982 with a degree in public relations, but—believe me—the public relations firms weren't exactly knocking at my door to give me a job. So around Christmas-time, I went down to the Mercantile Exchange and a college roommate of my brother who was a broker on the floor, brought me around to a few different companies on the floor, asking them if they needed a runner. Finally, I had an interview with a guy at Shatkin. I walked into his office and he asks me, 'What do you know about the business?' I figured I might as well be totally honest with the guy, so I said, 'Nothing. I have no idea what goes on here.' And then he says, 'O.K. You're hired.' I asked him if it was my resume that impressed him, but he said, 'Nope. You're Irish and you're from the south side of Chicago.' So the next week I started running in the bond room."

*Henry, twenty-five, started as a runner in December 1982. He worked at the Chicago Mercantile Exchange (CME), the Chicago Board of Trade (CBOT), and the Mid American Exchange (MidAm), in varying capacities, all for Shatkin Trading Co., a large local trading company. Today, he continues to do night outtrades for Shatkin, but during the day he works as a trader's assistant for one of the biggest treasury-bill traders at the CME. He is married, and at the time of the interview was earning about $20,000 a year, He's waiting anxiously for the day when his boss will help him buy or rent a membership, for which, as he says, "I just don't have the cash."*

"It's perfect to go to the Merc right out of college because you're used to being broke. If you only make $10,000 a year, you'll still have enough money to go out and have a beer. There's no way I could have come down here if I had a job first because it takes a while to learn the business. I don't know how guys work on the outside for, say, five years or whatever, making a decent buck—solid money—and then say, 'O.K. I'm going to go down to the Board of Trade and change everything.'

"It was good for me that I got into a small firm. Otherwise, I might not have participated in all the different things that I did. With a large firm, it might have taken a year or a year and a half before I could have even touched a phone.

"I got to do a hell of a lot in a very short time. In nine months, I worked in the currencies and T-bill pits at the Merc, the grain room at the Board and at the MidAm. I got to know the different characteristics of each market—T-bills, wheat, S & P's, and the currencies. After working as a runner in the currencies—six months total—I moved up to the main order desk as a phone clerk, which used to be in a back office. Customers would call us with the orders and then we'd call the floor. If someone put a big order in, we could check their margin to see if they had enough money. The customers wouldn't call in orders right on the market up to the order desk, so it was a good place for the novice to break in because, you figure, everybody's going to make mistakes to begin with. You also learned different things like what kind of orders you can put in.

"I had so much to learn. I would constantly be asking our phone clerks what was going on. What's that? What does that mean? Plus, the traders and brokers were usually pretty nice, and if you didn't understand something they would tell you what was what. You know, it's easy for a runner to learn because you really have a mindless job. There's not really that much to it. So it gave you a lot of time to sit tight and figure things out for yourself.

"After a year and a half as a runner, phone clerk, and trade checker, I had already learned most of the back office stuff—balancing books, checking trades, and that kind of thing—which I thought would help me in some small way when I began eventually to trade. But what I didn't know a lot about was what actually went on in the pit. It's funny. When you're on the floor, you've got an advantage over the guy on the street who's calling in. Then if you get a job in the pit with a broker or trader, you know a little more about what's going on in the pit than the guy who's working on the floor outside the pit. The things I pick up working near the pit are completely different from what I learned working outside the pit. Things like trading on the curb. That's hush-hush, but it goes on. Or scratching trades. The average Joe-Blow-customer doesn't really know how the pit works. But if you want to trade yourself, you got to know.

"It takes a while to learn this business. Yeah, there are people who buy memberships and go straight into the pit, but most of them disappear fast. There was a former football player with the Bears who had some money, came down here, and didn't know how to bid or offer. He's gone now. It's hard. Most people say you don't make any money in your first six months or year of trading.

"Also, I thought this job would help me get into the pit myself. I can't just jump from the street into the pit—I don't have the cash—so this is my way of working myself into the pit. Hopefully, it might be a way to get a loan so I can try trading for myself. My boss has already helped put two brothers in the pits, a brother-in-law, and a good friend. Besides that, going around and knowing the other traders and brokers in the pit is important. They know me now. I hope the way it works out is that if I ever get in there, they won't be afraid to trade with me. They'll know my trades will be good. And I may find that nice, little, cozy spot right next to one of the brokers someday and eat 1 lot orders all day. That'd be nice.

"If I started with a trader or broker, I might be in the pit right now. With two or three years under my belt with him, he might have decided I'm already ready for it. If you know a trader or broker, I'd definitely try to get in with them. A very well-rounded trader should know all the back office workings, but it's actually not necessary to make money in the pits. If you don't know anybody, you've got to go the traditional route, with a firm. The key is knowing somebody.

"A friend of mine who knew I wasn't happy working as a phone clerk, told me a friend of his, who was a big trader, was looking for a clerk. I didn't actually know the guy before he hired me, but I went over and talked to him. He told me what the job entailed: keeping his account, giving him his position constantly, and P and S'ing him all day long. He offered me the job, and I took it. The salary was about the same.

"What do I do for him? I get his statement in the morning and check what he did the day before: I see, maybe, that he's long 15 T-bills. I put that into my first count of the day and remind him that he's long 15 to start the day. Throughout the day, he hands me out his cards. On one card he may be long 40 bills, so now I add the 15 and he's long 55. I write on a card "long 55" and pass it back to him in the pit. He usually hands me out one or two cards at a time. Today, he did about 14,000 stuff—7,000 a side. So all day long I'm grabbing his cards. I also P & S it—to find out how many ticks he's up or down for the day. I also have to check the trades. Most of the trades are with brokers and large quantities and, for that reason, fairly easy to check. I go over to them and say, 'We sold you 200 at 6,' and they say, 'Yeah, good, we're Collins' or something like that. If he's put the wrong house, I'll change it. When you do 14,000 stuff, you're bound to to have a few mistakes. I put the month of the contract in, the time brackets, the handle on the price. Four or five times a day, he'll ask me what his money's at, so I'll send him a card up which shows how much he's up or down and where he's short them or long them. That's basically it.

"It's strange down here. A guy could be making a million dollars a year and talking to a runner who's making $150 a week, and it would be like you're talking to a regular guy. You don't wear anything that tells you how much money you make, unless you're wearing a Rolex or something. There's no pretension in the pit, really.

"The job warps you a little bit. My boss is real successful—no doubt about it. If he doesn't come in and make 1,000 ticks a day—now that's over $30,000—it's not a decent day. He'll come in and say, 'F---, I made only 300 ticks.' Now where's the perspective on that? You know, a 10 lot is a big trade, but when I've got 100 and 200 hundred and 400 hundred lots on my cards, I say, 'F--- the 10 lots; they'll be good; I'll check them later.' Money can't mean a whole lot to you down here. You got to be able to make it one day and blow it the next without going crazy. You know, if you talk with somebody on the outside and mention these numbers, there's no way they understand it. It seems impossible how someone can lose that much and make that much in one day.

"Today, for instance, I wanted to talk to my boss about a raise, and I'm not talking about a lot of money, maybe a hundred dollars more a week. Well, today he dropped $180,000. What's another hundred bucks a week for me? But he knows how tough it is to make that money; he doesn't like giving any of it back.

"He was in the same boat I'm in. He's been at the Merc five years and is now thirty years old. His cousin was down here, and his cousin gave him the money—a T-bill, I think—to put in his account. He began trading with $10,000 and didn't make any money until the last couple months of his first year trading, and then made like $100,000 and increased it every year.

"He was a grocery guy at Jewel—the one who sprays the vegetables down and s--- like that. He would trade during the day and do that at night. Even after he was making huge amounts of money, he never quit his Jewel job. He'd be making $200,000 a year or whatever, and he still kept his Jewel job.

"What really p----- you off is when you see a guy work for someone for, maybe, three or four months. They may have a good rap with the guy and, maybe, they're buddies on the outside. And poof—the next thing you know the guy's in the pit, making a ton of money, and he doesn't know anything about the business—at least that's what I'm thinking. I know it's just jealousy, though.

"Of course, there's been times when I want to say forget it—it's not worth it being beat up on all day, getting yelled at, getting spit on. But, then, I don't know if I could ever go back to sitting behind a desk and pushing papers around. I'd be fired, I think, the first day because of the way you talk after being down here so long. You tell some guy, 'F--- you' or 'Yea, sure, I'll get back to you.' I do have a goal set that by this January, I want to be in the pit. I don't know if it's possible, but that's what I want."

# *Andy*

"I worked for a steel company—Ryerson Steel in Chicago—for four years and then they laid me off. I was on unemployment for a while, and I had friends at the Merc who said I should try coming down here. But I was making more money on unemployment than I would be making if I came down here to run. So I kept on putting it off, saying, 'Oh, I'll find something better.' But pretty soon six months had gone by and I hadn't found anything, so I said, 'Hell, I'll get my feet wet.'"

*Andy came down to the Chicago Mercantile Exchange (CME) when he was twenty-four. A college graduate from DePaul University in Chicago, he started running in early 1981 with a large retail brokerage house. He worked as a runner, phone clerk, and trade checker for nine months before leaving to work for a smaller local clearing house as a phone clerk at their treasury bill desk. For the last twenty months, he's done night outtrades for that firm and during the day works as a broker's assistant in the bond pit. Like many young people in the business who do not have the money to buy or lease a membership for themselves, he is putting in his time as a broker's assistant, with the hope that his bosses will help him get into the pit when they think he's ready. As Andy says, "They've told me they are going to—it's just a matter of time."*

"So I came down here and started running for a large firm. I had no exposure to this business before I came down here. I first thought when they said someone had a seat on the Merc—and they mentioned the pit—that the place was like a big auditorium, shaped like a pit, with seats. And this guy had his seat and another guy his other spot. And both of them go there and sit down everyday.

"My impression was that it was more of a private club and that there was no sense coming down here because it was a family business.

"There were four or five of my friends down here. So I just went in, and my friends told me what companies to try to start with. Commercial houses, they said, were much easier to get a job in because they're the ones that need the runners. They're the ones with the customer business—the phone calls coming in—and the orders got to get into the pit to the broker somehow, so they're the ones that need the runners. A local firm has traders in the pit who trade for themselves all day long. They don't need any runners.

"Basically, someone was just helping me out. I had a friend and he told them, 'Listen, I've got a friend here who I want to get in.' It was lucky they needed a runner. I was in the right place at the right time. I also put in applications all over.

"Everybody who comes into this business is going to step into a runner's job. Because there's nothing you can go to college for or anything like that to teach you this business. I mean, it's like going to school when you come down here.

"You couldn't just walk from the street and expect to begin trading. People do, of course. But you've got to get to know people—know what's going on, and know all the different firms. What else is essential? The different kinds of orders. What a stop is. You have to learn those things. Etiquette in the pit, too. You can't jump in front of people. If someone makes a market, you've got to respect that person's market. You can't jump in front of his trade. It just takes a little time to learn how the business is.

"I'm not saying it can't be done—that you can't just walk off the street and start trading. If you've got the money to burn, I suppose you can. And you'll learn eventually. But for the average person, who doesn't have the money, it's better to come down here and start slowly.

"So I ran for probably five months in the grains and then I became a phone clerk and learned outtrades as a trade checker. But before I began trade checking, because I was a little older than the average runner, they were nice enough to give me a little more time to pick up a little extra money. So I'd come in about 7:30, get stuff ready, and then they kept me about an hour or an hour and a half after the close doing other stuff, just to try and put some hours in.

"They started their runners off at four dollars an hour, but because I had some college behind me they started me off at five. And I stayed with that for a while until they put me on salary. Salary, I think, was only about $11,000 a year. I had to be down here between 6:30 and 7:00 and stayed until 2:00. The pay never got any better. Then I started shopping around down here. Once I had some experience, I could look for another job.

"You start meeting people down here and hear of openings in other places. I met some people down here who were working for another firm and they had an opening. So I started talking to them about outtrades and told them I had a year under my belt doing outtrrades. I quit my old job and came to the new firm for about a $5,000 increase. I think I started at $16,000 at the time, checking their outtrades and working at their T-bills desk. It was a 6:30 to 2:00 job.

"This business is centered around meeting people. It's the biggest part of the business. Making the right connections means almost everything. How do you think those people in the pit got in the pit? Someone got them in there. Either they're from money and through their family had the money to go in there and buy a membership, or a firm has put them in there, or another trader that they have worked for or come to know has bought them a membership and got them in the pit. I mean, they didn't just come with the membership. They had to get help somehow. Either you had the money to do it yourself, which probably very few people do, or someone backed you in doing it.

"I was working at the bill desk, but I didn't work there that long. When they took me off the nights, I didn't think I was making enough money, so I went looking for a job in the evening doing someone else's night outs. But the firm didn't want me to do that. They said it was against company rules or something. So they offered me a deal of just working mornings and evenings and being off during the day. That allowed me to go look on the floor for a clerk job with someone. Since I had experience by this time, it wasn't that tough finding one. Plus, I hit one of the guys who was our own broker who I already knew pretty well anyway. He gave me a job as a broker's assistant. A broker's assistant isn't really something you can just walk into. You've got to have a little bit of experience before you do it.

"It's hard at first because they say there's a lot of money going around down here, exchanging hands, but for the first few years, you can't expect to be making too much of it. They can get anybody off the street to do the job you're going to be doing for the next few years. When you start to know enough and have experience, and they can't just go get a kid off the street to replace you, you'll start to see some money.

"I'm working until one these guys buys me a membership or gives me enough money that I can lease a membership. I have to wait until the guys I work for are ready to put me in there. They've told me they are going to—it's just a matter of time.

"You put your time in with people and some are a little quicker with getting it for you. But basically, it's almost kind of expected: put your time in and they'll get you in there. Because some one helped get them in there. They're just passing it down the line.

"There's guys down here whose clerks have been here no more than four or five months, and now they're in the pits trading. It all depends on the personality of the trader you work for.

"The ideal way? I think it's what I'm doing. I can't afford to get myself in there. To learn outtrades is going to help a lot. Because you want to know what's going on with your money. And you want to know when someone's screwing you around with an outtrade. Also, the trade checker gets to meet a lot of the traders and brokers, and that helps, especially in this business. And being a clerk for someone is, I think, the best final step into the pit. Hopefully, the people you work for have enough money and believe in you enough to help you get in there."

# 4

---

# Memberships:
# How To Get One When
# You Don't Have Dough

---

If you've got the money, obtaining a membership is easy. At most exchanges, you need only to submit a financial statement, take a short introductory course on trading, pass a simple test on exchange rules, and have two exchange members sponsor your application—a very easy process. The final step for approval involves making a personal appearance before an official body of exchange members. Sounds menacing? It isn't. The review process is meant to sort out a few bad apples, not to make obtaining a membership difficult. Assuming you haven't served time for securities fraud, embezzled large sums of money, or passed counterfeit money, the exchanges want you. They are open to anyone who can afford it.

But what if you can't afford it? What if you are part of the 99 percent of the population that, by some quirk of fate, doesn't have a spare $200,000 to buy a full membership at the Chicago Board of Trade (CBOT) or $148,000 to buy a membership on the International Monetary Markets

(IMM) at the Chicago Mercantile Exchange (CME) or even $30,000 to buy a commodity options membership at the CBOT? What do you do if you're a twenty-seven-year-old who has worked hard and wants to begin trading but just hasn't been able to save that kind of cash?

### I Can Always Lease a Membership, Right?

Wrong. It's true that you can lease memberships, and it used to be that leasing a membership was a good alternative to buying one, but the days of leasing memberships are numbered. In the past, a young kid could rent a small seat at the CBOT at a reasonable price—say $200 a month for a Commodity Option Market (COM) membership—and begin trading with as little as $5,000 in his account. But the exchanges are making it increasingly more difficult for the little guy to begin a trading career, and the stipulations for leasing a membership are becoming more strict. The larger exchanges are slowly becoming more and more like those posh fifth avenue boutiques that cater exclusively to the rich and close their doors to the general public. Today, the larger exchanges require heavy capitalization—a $50,000 minimum in all accounts at the CBOT, a $100,000 minimum at the Commodity Exchange, Inc. (COMEX), in New York, and a $25,000 minimum at the CME. This means that leasing a membership has become almost as difficult for a young person as buying one.

### Why the Change?

Three reasons: First, at the larger exchanges, the small undercapitalized trader is now a burden where before he was the bread-and-butter of exchange trading. It's the price of success. The successful exchanges need well-capitalized individuals who can shoot big numbers. The kid with $5,000 in his account only crowds the exchange floor. His 1 and 2 lot trades no longer provide the necessary liquidity for the larger exchanges to maintain efficient markets.

Second, some people abused the leasing privileges. People would lease cheap memberships solely as a way to avoid paying high commissions. They might never even trade in the commodity for which the membership was issued. For example, at the CBOT people leased COM memberships for $200 a month—an average of $6 a day—and opened a trading account with a local brokerage firm. Instead of trading commodity options, for which the membership was designated, they would stand outside the bond and wheat pits all day handing orders to brokers, thus taking full advantage of the cheap commission rates afforded floor traders. A 1 lot trade in the bond pit might cost the average outside customer $20, but it costs a floor trader $4 at most—a $16 savings on just a 1 lot. Multiply the savings by twenty or thirty times every day and you can see the advantages and possible abuses of renting a cheap membership.

Third, many full members of most exchanges don't feel that lessees, as a rule, make a sufficient committment to the exchanges. Lessees are around in the good times, but the moment the markets slow down, they leave. Lessees crowd the trading pits, which means that full members often can't find a good spot in the pits. It didn't used to be like that. The growth in contracts has fragmented the industry. No longer are there just four or five pits in which a steady flow of orders is almost guaranteed. Outside customers have many more options today, and the result is that the trading activity of different pits rises and falls depending on the economy and the market mood. Full members want easier access to all the pits, and many feel that reducing, if not entirely eliminating, leasing privileges will help them get it.

### How Do You Buy a Membership?

Just like the commodities traded at the various U.S. exchanges, memberships are bought and sold on a bid and offer basis. There is no set price for buying a seat at, say, the

CME. Prices fluctuate depending on the latest bid and offer. In 1964 a seat at the CME cost $3,000; in November 1980 a seat traded at $380,000; and in August 1985 a seat was offered at $160,000. The price of a seat is highest when markets are busy and trading is active. At the end of World War II, the markets were dead because of government price supports, and a seat at the CBOT cost $25. A full seat at the CBOT costs approximately $200,000 today.

Most exchanges offer a selection of memberships, each of which allows its holder to trade different commodities. For example:

### Chicago Board of Trade

| Membership | Trading Privileges | Approximate Seat Cost-1986 |
|---|---|---|
| Full | All Commodities | $191,000 |
| Associate | All Commodities, except Grain & Silver Futures | $80,000 |
| IDEM | 1-Kilo Gold, Major Market Index | $20,000 |
| COM | All Options | $30,000 |
| GIM | GNMA-CDR, T-Bonds, T-Notes, GNMA II | $47,000 |

### Chicago Mercantile Exchange

| Membership | Trading Privileges | Approximate Seat Cost/Lease1986 |
|---|---|---|
| Full | All Contracts | $160,000/$2,000 |
| IMM | All Contracts except Meat Futures | $148,000/$1,800 |
| IOM | All Index & Options Contracts plus Lumber Futures | $52,000/$525 |

## What Are the Alternatives to Buying or Leasing Membership for Oneself?

In the past, there have been four ways someone who couldn't afford a membership found a way into the trading pits: (1) individual assistance; (2) partnerships; (3) working for a firm that hires traders; and (4) beginning at a small exchange where the cost of admission is relatively inexpensive. I'll describe each of these four paths, but I will also look toward the future. Changing markets mean changing opportunities. I'll try to anticipate certain market changes and show you how you might benefit from them.

When you get serious about obtaining a job or a seat, the best places to get detailed information are the exchanges themselves. Either write to them, or better yet, visit their administrative offices. Ask them for literature and manuals. In most cases they have this material and will be glad to supply it. Their addresses and phone numbers appear in chapter 1.

### Individuals

The most common way for a young person to get into the pits is to work for a trader or broker who will help buy or finance a membership. It takes time. You have to pay your dues, build up someone's trust and prove your competence, but older traders helping younger traders into the pits is part of the commodities business. As Andy, a twenty-seven-year-old broker's assistant told me, "You put your time in with people, and some are a little quicker with getting it for you. But basically, it's almost kind of expected: put your time in and they'll get you in there. Because someone helped get them in there. They're just passing it down the line."

Occasionally, traders and brokers will buy their clerks a membership outright, but most help in other ways. Some members help finance a membership by loaning their clerks the money to buy one. Others may help a clerk lease a membership by putting the $50,000 or $100,000 capitalization requirement in the face of a T-bill in their clerk's account. And, at the CBOT, many members own 1/4 and 1/2 memberships, which they have been known to give to their clerks to help them get started, or sell at favorable terms to them.

Of course, paying your dues isn't always fun. A clerk may work for a broker or trader for two or three years before help is offered, and the wait can be painful. But no matter how frustrating, it's usually worth it. Broker's and trader's assistant positions are in high demand. If you can get in with a broker or trader and make him or her believe in you, there's a good chance you'll receive help getting into the pit. In chapter 3, Steve, who worked as a trader's assistant for nine months before beginning trading, found that approach worked for him: "Guys would have worked for free to do what I did: to stand behind some guy, get along with him, and hope they get set up with him. In fact, when I left the guy, they were all dying for my old job."

## Partnerships

Partnerships are more common at the options exchanges than in futures, but they exist in both. Basically, it's an agreement between two parties, a young person without any money who has worked at the exchange for some time and a well-established individual who hopes to profit by financially backing the beginning trader. The agreement is simple: the backer sets the person up with a membership and a trading account with a certain amount of capital, and the trader agrees to split trading profits fifty-fifty or some other agreed upon amount. Sometimes, partnerships are casual agreements. A friend may want to give a trader a chance to trade on his or her own by offering the trader a certain amount of money as a loan. The two will then make an agreement that splits the profits and permits the new trader to buy his or her way out at any time. But most partnerships are more serious. One individual may back eight or ten different traders at a time. The established trader may have half a million dollars or more tied up backing young traders. Each new trader makes a commitment to trade only for the backer for a specified period of time, usually two years.

Partnerships are a mixed bag, and young traders must be careful when entering into one. When the agreements are casual and offered out of friendship, they can be a good opportunity. The backer rarely makes any money because as soon as the trader begins to make money the backer will be bought out, but the backer knows that. As Scott explained in chapter 3, "I bought him out after eight months. He wasn't too happy about it 'cuz he was taking the big risk—ten grand. But he made about five grand on the deal, which in less than a year is 60 percent return. He couldn't really complain financially. He came out alright."

The stricter agreements, however, can cause more serious problems. These partnerships are generally a heads-I-win-tails-you-lose deal. The new trader doesn't like it because as soon as he or she starts making money, the backer starts pulling out chunks of money. The backer doesn't like it because the new trader usually wants out of the deal as soon as money starts to be made. Each one of them is always watching the other's hands. Also some backers have a hard time giving their traders breathing space—space that every beginning trader desperately needs. With these backers, if the traders don't make money right away, they'll dump them. This can be devastating to a young trader who then is without a job and, probably worse, filled with serious doubts about his or her trading ability.

## How Firms Hire

At all major exchanges, some firms hire young people to trade for them. Each firm works differently, but most firms pay their traders a flat fee—enough so they don't have to worry about paying the rent or eating—plus a yearly bonus. This usually is either a percentage of trading profits on a graduated scale or a percentage of the firm's overall profits.

For example, traders might receive 30 percent of the first $100,000 they make, 50 percent of the second $100,000, and 70 percent of the third.

In Chicago, the most successful of these types of companies—Trade-link CRT, and Singer-Wenger—are most heavily involved in options on futures both at the CBOT and the CME. Options are a slower, more methodical, and probably a more strategic game than futures, and it's easier for a firm to train and keep a close eye on its traders in the options pits than in the futures pit.

Trading for a company has its disadvantages. A trader is at the mercy of a firm. It's not like being a local. Trader decisions are often made by a stategist in the back office who tells them what to do during the course of the day—for example, buy a spread at this particular price and sell it at a different price or buy calls at this volatility and sell them at that volatility. Different firms allow their traders varying degrees of independence, but trading for a firm can be limiting.

Trading for a company also has tremendous advantages. You won't have to worry about financing a membership. Different firms work in different ways, but the standard method is to transfer a company's seat into the trader's name. A trader doesn't have to pay anything. In chapter 3, Mike, who trades bond options for Singer-Wenger, put it this way: "Singer-Wenger backs me financially. It's their money that I'm trading. I'm a salaried broker for them. It's their membership. I don't have to pay a thing. I'm just the managerial nominee." In other words, his personal financial risk is zero. The only thing that he can lose is his job.

Firms are also good because they eliminate some of the initial fear of being a beginning trader. A trading firm might have five or six traders in one pit, and while you're not exactly brothers, traders tend to look out for one another, especially if their bonus depends on the firm's overall profits. Most firms also provide their beginning traders with extensive training in trading strategy.

### Are There Opportunities at Smaller Exchanges?

Yes. One of the best ways to begin a trading career is at a smaller exchange, like the Mid American Commodity Exchange (MidAm) in Chicago. It's a matter of simple economics. Most young people are undercapitalized, and the entrance fee at a small exchange is usually the price of the membership—$5,000 at the MidAm with no additional capitalization requirements. You're not likely to become rich at the MidAm, but you don't go there to make your fortune. You go there to learn how to trade. As Jim, who began his career at the MidAm before moving to the CBOT, described in chapter 3, "the tuition is a lot cheaper at the MidAm. The contracts are half the size as the Board's or the Merc's. So if you screw-up, it'll only cost you half as much."

Don't be fooled: Nobody's giving you a $200,000 seat for $5,000. Compared to the larger exchanges, the liquidity—that is, the level of trading activity—just isn't there. So while you'll be able to trade as big and as often as you want, you probably won't be able to get out of your trades as easily as you'd like. Some of the CBOT's and CME's best and most famous traders began their careers at the MidAm, and many traders make nice livings there. It's a more difficult place to make money because of the lack of customer orders, but, as one twenty-seven-year-old bond trader at the CBOT told me, "I've never seen someone who was successful at the MidAm come to the Board of Trade and lose money. It's a great—no, it's the best—training ground for young traders."

### What's Around the Corner?

This book can't predict the future, but it's extremely important for anyone entering the commodity industry now to understand its changing face. Many knowledgeable people in the industry believe that trading companies are the way of the future. In the next ten years, large corporate pools of money probably will come to maintain the markets. The independent trader will become a dinosaur. Capital requirements will become so large that pools of money—for example, maybe eight or ten traders with $10 million behind them—will become the trading standard.

The situation is this: five years ago, a 1,000 lot in the treasury bond pit was a rare occurrence, but today it's not an unreasonable amount. In 1982, only thirteen of the top two-hundred pension funds used futures, but in 1984 forty used them. This is still only about 20 percent and the percentage is significantly less for the total number of U.S. pension funds, but the trend is there. Currently, large money managers are not using futures speculatively. But this will surely change with time. Finally, the 1, 2, and 5-lot players of a few years ago are today putting their money into commodity funds—probably a smart move considering the benefits of expert management, lower commissions, and constant market surveillance.

Large pools of corporate money means more sophisticated players, which also changes the nature of the game. The local pit traders who make their living off the 20 and 30 bean orders in the soybean pit or the local who eats 5 lot orders in the bond pit all day at the CBOT can't do it anymore. If you want to be near a broker in the bond pit today, you have to trade 100 lots. In the 70's and early 80's, a trader could become rich feeding off the small, outside orders. But it's almost impossible to do that today. The guys shooting 100 lots into the bond pit aren't like the doctors and lawyers in the past who traded 5 lots. They are sophisticated traders usually taking advantage of arbitrage opportunities.

But what does it mean? It means that if you understand the changes likely to occur, you will be able to take advantage of them. In the future, the individual trader who isn't sufficiently capitalized will be lost. Having $50,000 or $100,000 in an account won't mean anything. The size of an average trade in the bond pit might be 50 or 100 lots. The bottom line will be that to make money a trader will have to trade large amounts. The goal is to get closer and closer to paper (the traders' term for customer orders). The closer you are to paper, the larger the edge is. The kid with $50,000 who is trading 5 lots will be so far from the paper that he won't be able to make any money. A trading firm with, maybe, $5 million of capital behind it will allow traders to trade 50 lots.

It's not that working for a company is better than trading independently. It's probably not. The best situation possible is to be an independent trader—be your own boss, work when you want, leave when you want, no arguments, and no profits to split. But in the future, working for a trading company may not be a question of personal preference but one of survival. Without the capitalization of a trading firm, most traders won't be able to trade 50 or 100 lots on their own. What good is it to be your own boss if you can't make any money?

# 5

# The First Job: How To Get It

My old method of job hunting was probably the best. Whenever I wanted a summer job on the floor during high school or college, I asked my dad, "Dad, can you get me a job?" It didn't take any effort on my part, and since my dad was a trader, it worked every time. But what if your dad isn't a trader? How difficult is it to to get a foot in the door? And what exactly does it take to get a job?

To find out exactly what you need to do to get a job, I went to the Chicago Mercantile Exchange (CME) in late July to find one. I used a friend's resume, pretending I was a college graduate from the University of Wisconsin, who had no previous experience in the business. I did not want to take advantage of my experience or connections. I pretended I knew no one at the exchange. I even chose a bad time to go job hunting—the summer being the worst time to find a job because most firms are flooded with summer help.

I had no idea how long it would take. I figured at least a

couple of days.

I landed a job after an hour and a half.

I was surprised. If I hadn't made things difficult for myself by not being able to get on the floor, I would have found one even faster. Let's retrace my steps.

### Where to Start?

I knew beforehand that the best way to land a job is to walk around the trading floor, stop at individual firms' desks, and ask if they have any openings. I also knew that to get on the floor of an exchange, a member of the exchange has to sign you on. But any young person, with a little initiative, can get onto the trading floor. I was tempted on several occasions to explain my situation to any one of the young traders I saw and then ask them if they would sign me on the floor. I didn't, but don't let that stop you. It's worth a try.

Why is it so important to get on the floor? In most firms, the person who does the hiring is the floor manager. It's the floor manager who knows if the firm needs someone, and it's the floor manager who does the interviewing. In my search for a job, I limited myself to going around to the offices of the firms. If the floor manager was there, I was in luck, but most floor managers spend the whole day on the floor. As a result, I talked to a lot of secretaries who had no power to hire me. On two occasions, the secretary asked me to fill out an employment application and leave my resume, promising to give both to the floor manager. But that's not the way to get a job. You can't expect to be hired if you leave an employee application and a resume. You have to meet the floor manager, look him or her straight in the eye, and make it clear you want a job. Then, if your timing is right and there's a job opening, you have made things very easy for the floor manager. Instead of searching through a pile of resumes and job applications, you can be hired on the spot. As you'll see, it's how I got my job.

## What Should I Wear?

The commodity exchanges present an interesting twist to job hunting. If I were being interviewed for a job at a bank or law firm, I would wear a nice suit and tie. But in searching for a job at the CME, I intentionally underdressed. I wore a buttoned shirt and nice pants and loafers, but I didn't wear a jacket or tie.

Why? The commodity exchanges are not a major center of high fashion. The majority of traders wear polo shirts with a tie loosely draped around the neck, and many wear tennis shoes, although at some exchanges tennis shoes are prohibited. Most exchanges have a dress code requiring all traders to wear "proper" business attire, including a tie, but fashion still isn't a major concern on the floor.

## Should I Bring a Resume?

It's not absolutely necessary, but you probably should have one. Otherwise you don't have anything to show your prospective employer, which means you have nothing to distinguish you from the other job hunters. A copy of the resume I used follows.

Notice it has nothing to do with commodities. Todd never even took an economics course in college. The resume is directed towards management training and sales. But that's the point. There is no correct preparation for a career in commodities. Your past experience is practically irrelevent when it comes to finding a job at an exchange. Nobody cares where or what you studied. In fact, looking over the resume, the floor manager at Paine Webber who hired me said she was glad to see that I hadn't had *any* experience in the business because Paine Webber liked to train their employees from scatch.

TODD H. FELDMAN
_____

73 Lakeside Place
Highland Park, IL 60035
312/433-0333

OBJECTIVE
A position that will utilize my strong background in communications, public relations, project coordinating experience while providing career development with management potential.

EDUCATION
University of Wisconsin, Madison Wisconsin
Bachelor of Arts

PROFESSIONAL EXPERIENCE
Successfully represented products to consumers. Substantial experience handling customer service problems, consumer complaints, and sales service. Solicited business from clients to develop account profile.

Responsible for sales, inventory control, accounting and management for retail outlet store.

Developed, instituted and managed own specialized business, including but not limited to, establishing and developing accounts, labor and servicing of customers needs and sales.

PROFESSIONAL HISTORY
1983 - 1984:  C.P.I.
Sales Representative

1982 - 1983:  Bake Rite Bakery
Sales Representative/Manager

1979 - 1981:  Self Employed

1977 - 1979:  Ravinia Hardware
Sales Clerk

ORGANIZATIONS/ACTIVITIES
University of Wisconsin/Pre-Law Society
University of Wisconsin/Intramural Club

Professional Sports, Intramural Basketball and Baseball, Reading

PERSONAL
Available Immediately

STRENGTHS
Evaluated as a high achiever...energetic, outgoing personality... strong persuasive skills

REFERENCES
Available upon request.

### Where Are the Firms?

The first thing I did upon entering the Mercantile Exchange building was ask the guard at the information desk where the library was. I knew that most large exchanges have their own libraries, and I figured that was the logical place to find a list of all of the firm names who trade at the Merc and their office numbers. I was wrong. The librarian said she didn't have anything like that, but said the clearing corporation on the sixth floor might.

I figured I needed a list of firms because I didn't want to wander aimlessly through the building looking for the offices of different brokerage firms. I thought a list would bring some order to my search by helping me keep track of where I had been and what I had done. Fortunately, the clearing corporation had just what I wanted: a complete list of all the clearing firms, with their office location and the name of each firm's office manager.

I started my search in a haphazard way. I didn't care where I got my first job. It didn't matter to me whether I worked for a large national brokerage house or a small local firm. I just wanted to get my foot in the door and then, if I didn't like the company, I could easily find something else once I was on the floor.

So for no logical reason, except that the first clearing house on the list was First Options Futures on the seventeenth floor, I took the elevator up. Unfortunately, I couldn't find First Options Futures' office, but there were several other brokerage offices on the same floor.

I stopped first at Transmarket Group, Inc. I had never heard of the firm, but I didn't care. It was the third name on the list, and if they needed a runner, what did it matter if I had never heard of them? So taking a deep breath, I opened the door and prepared myself to smile nicely at the secretary, tell her politely I was interested in applying for a position as a runner, and ask her kindly if I could speak to the floor manager. But, to my surprise, the office was empty—furnished, but the lights were off, and no one was there. I immediately thought that this could be a very long day.

There were many offices with company names on them, but I didn't want to walk into offices randomly. I couldn't be sure if they were brokerage firms or not. So if I saw a name which I had never heard of, I checked to see if it was on the clearing house list. If it wasn't, I passed by.

My next stop was also on the seventeenth floor at Lind Waldock & Co., a firm that I had heard of before but didn't really know much about, except that they were also at the Chicago Board of Trade (CBOT). It was my first of several hard hits against the wall. I introduced myself to the secretary, told her I was interested in applying for a position as a runner, and asked her if I could speak to the floor manager, assuming, I said, that he was the one who did the firm's hiring. Smiling, she said she was sorry, but the floor manager was on the floor right now. She suggested—between phone calls, of course—that I leave my resume with her and she would give it to him. Fine, I said, but could I also leave a note for him. For some reason, I thought a personal note would catch his attention. I asked the receptionist for his name and wrote a short note telling him I knew the summer was a bad time to find a job, but that I was willing to start in September. I said I looked forward to hearing from him. On reflection, it was a nonproductive idea, but I hadn't quite learned yet that friendly notes and friendly secretaries were not going to get me a job.

Next, I took the elevator down to the eleventh floor because I noticed that many of the firms on the list were located there. My third, fourth, fifth, and sixth attempts were much the same as the second. I stopped first at Shatkin, one of the largest brokerage firms at both the CBOT and the CME. I accidentally walked into the firm's back office but eventually made my way to the receptionist in front, where I introduced myself, said I was looking for a job, and asked to see the floor manager. Once again, I was politely told that the floor manager was busy on the floor, but that I could fill out an employee's application and leave my resume, which she would give him "as soon as he came up."

I filled everything out, but I was becoming frustrated. It doesn't take long to realize that without seeing the floor manager, you're not going anywhere. Up to this point, I didn't know whether any of the firms I had visited needed help now or in September.

I stopped next at G.H. Miller. I had never heard of the firm before, but it was on the list and right next to Shatkin's office. I didn't get a job there either, but at least they offered a little variety: the receptionist was a witch, who didn't even let me leave my resume. Even before I finished introducing myself, she snapped at me, "We're not hiring anybody!"

Next, I stopped at Singer-Wenger, a trading company, which turned out to be almost an exact replay of going to Shatkin: I was polite, the receptionist was polite, the floor manager wasn't there, but would I kindly fill out these employee application forms and, oh yes, leave your resume, too.

I took the elevator up to the twelfth floor and stopped at another firm I had never heard of, Western Trading. I gave the receptionist my spiel, expecting her to give me an employee application, but I didn't even get that far. She told me that Western Trading had just taken over two smaller firms and that they had to lay off people, not hire them.

Finally, after six attempts and realizing I wasn't getting anywhere, I got lucky and came across a good way to see a firm's floor manager without being on the exchange floor.

I accidentally walked into the back office of Gelderman-Peavy, a large retail brokerage house at the Merc. I was looking for the front office, where I could apply for a job, but because I misread the room number on the list of names I had, I walked into the clearing room where the keypunchers recorded the days' trades. I asked them if they knew of any openings in the firm, and they said I should talk to their floor manager, Frank Young. I said, "Great, but where is he?"

They told me to go down to the guest's desk on the trading floor and page him. It was the perfect solution. If you don't know anybody to get you on the exchange floor, you can always page a trader to come off the floor. I should have thought of doing it long before. At the front desk, I could introduce myself to him, tell him I was looking for a job, and ask him if he had anything. There was the risk that he might be busy and wouldn't like being paged, but it was 11:30 a.m., which is a slow time for most markets, and, besides, when someone on the floor is busy they usually won't hear or acknowledge their pages.

It worked perfectly. He appeared at the front desk in less than a minute. I apologized for paging him, but he didn't seem to be bothered. I introduced myself, told him I was looking for a job, and said I knew he was the person to talk to. He said that they didn't need anybody right now. I asked if they might after summer when the summer help goes back to school. He said probably not because they were overstaffed now anyway, but he wasn't sure. He took a copy of my resume, gave me his card, and told me to call him come September 1, if I still needed a job. It took about thirty seconds, but at least I had some real information.

Get in touch with the floor manager and then you'll know if the firm is hiring or if they will be in the future. Otherwise, you're knocking you're head against the wall. Secretaries may be very nice, but leaving your resume with them doesn't give you any clue as to whether you might get a job. Find out the name of the firm's floor manager and page him or her. Fortunately, I didn't have to do that again because I found a job on my next effort.

On the elevator ride back up to knock on some more doors, I started talking to a runner. I told her I was looking for a job and asked her if she knew anybody who was hiring. She said she worked for Paine Webber and that they had been hiring people all summer and that their office was on the eleventh floor.

Paine Webber must have just moved in because their name wasn't even on a door. But through a glass door, I could see some green jackets with the Paine Webber emblem on them, so I walked in. Three young people were sitting there in trading jackets. I asked, "Where should I go if I want to apply for a job?" And the one woman there immediately said she was the floor manager and did the firm's hiring. Before I even introduced myself, she said that her one stipulation for employment was that the person she hired had to be a college graduate. I said I was.

She introduced herself, asked me if I had a resume, looked it over briefly, and asked me what I was looking for from a job down here. I said that I wanted a chance to learn about the business, start at the bottom and work myself up the ladder. She asked me what I knew about the business. I said, "absolutely nothing" and, as I expected, she said, "Good. Paine Webber likes to train their own people anyway." Then she asked me how I knew about the business. I said I had a friend who was a trader at the CBOT and a friend who ran at the Merc. She asked me what I was doing now. I said I was working as an usher at night at Ravinia Park, a summer music festival near my home, and that because I worked at night I could start my job as soon as possible. I don't really think she read the resume very closely. I do think, however, she was impressed that I was professional enough to have one. Anyway, she then started telling me about the pay and benefits— $9,500 a year, which averages to $183 a week, "really high," she said "for a runner's job," plus dental, hospital, and medical benefits. She mentioned a few other firms' starting salaries, which hovered closer to $125 a week.

Finally, she started laughing and said to the other two people who were in the room, "I don't hire people off the cuff, do I?" She said the job was mine, if I wanted it, and she wanted to know when I could start. I told her in a couple of weeks, but I got the feeling I could have started the next day if I had wanted to. She said my day would be six hours long from 7:00 a.m. to 1:00 p.m. and that as I acquired experience, my hours would increase. Next I waited for a packet of forms to be filled out by all new employees, and that was it. She told me to meet her in that office at 7:00 a.m. on August 5.

If I were just starting out, I would have been on my way. Let's hope you find the right first job—right away—but don't be discouraged if it takes a while.

Good luck.

# Appendix

## TOTAL FUTURES VOLUME*

| Year | Volume | Year | Volume |
|------|--------|------|--------|
| 1970 | 13,622,607 | 1978 | 58,462,172 |
| 1971 | 14,563,331 | 1979 | 75,966,471 |
| 1972 | 18,329,643 | 1980 | 92,096,109 |
| 1973 | 25,826,747 | 1981 | 98,522,371 |
| 1974 | 27,733,328 | 1982 | 112,400,879 |
| 1975 | 32,200,103 | 1983 | 139,924,940 |
|      |            | 1984 | 149,086,938 |

*Does not include options on futures

Months

January = F
February = G
March = H
April = J
May = K
June = M
July = N
August = Q
September = U
October = V
November = X
December = Z

Commodities

Corn = C
Soybeans = S
Treasury Bonds = US
Ginnae Mae = M
Silver = SI
Gold = KI
Pork Bellies = PB
Hogs = LH
Oats = O
Wheat = W
Crude Oil = BO
Sugar = SU

### EXCHANGE VOLUME
*including options on futures*

| Exchange* | 1980 | 1981 | 1982 | 1983 | 1984 |
|---|---|---|---|---|---|
| CBT | 45,281,571 | 49,085,763 | 48,325,562 | 64,476,444 | 74,377,130 |
| CME | 22,261,295 | 24,527,020 | 33,574,286 | 38,111,134 | 44,585,635 |
| COMEX | 11,009,389 | 13,293,049 | 17,577,448 | 20,401,098 | 19,979,395 |
| NYME | 1,154,905 | 1,781,407 | 2,649,941 | 3,926,585 | 5,344,995 |
| CSC | 4,886,416 | 3,562,613 | 3,254,354 | 4,883,652 | 4,197,842 |
| NYFE | 183,993 | 290,585 | 1,451,442 | 3,816,887 | 3,703,157 |
| MIDAM | 2,993,636 | 2,588,540 | 2,397,721 | 3,166,537 | 3,104,322 |
| KCBOT | 1,298,047 | 1,181,884 | 1,493,558 | 1,693,210 | 1,898,681 |
| NYCE | 2,653,294 | 1,802,891 | 1,479,781 | 1,703,105 | 1,479,588 |
| MGE | 360,979 | 372,624 | 346,264 | 379,607 | 341,356 |
| CRCE | | | | 13,542 | 2,978 |

*See pp. 11-12 for key to abbreviations.

### *Types of Orders*

**Market Order:**  States quantity and commodity description and is to be executed at best possible price when order reaches trading pit.

**Price Limit Order:**  Contains a price limitation specified by the customer. It can be executed only at the price specified or at a better price.

**Fill or Kill Order:**  Specifies a price at which the order becomes similar to a market order and is executed at the best possible price. A stop order to buy is placed at a price above the prevailing market price and is not to be executed until the price advances to or above the stop price. At this point it becomes a market order and will be executed at the best possible price. A stop order to sell is placed at a price below the prevailing market. The order becomes a market order the instant the stop price is reached and will then be executed at the best possible price.

**Stop Limit Order:**  Differs from a stop order in that when the market reaches the specified stop price, the order becomes a limit order as opposed to a market order. A buy stop limit must be executed at or below the limit. A sell stop limit must be executed at a price at or above the limit.

**Market If Touched Order**  May be executed only if the market reaches a specified point. An MIT to buy becomes a market order if and when the commodity sells at or below the order price, and an MIT order to sell becomes a market order if and when the commodity reaches a specified or higher price.

**Market On Close Order:** Contains commodity and option to buy or sell and can only be executed within the closing range of that day's trading.

**Contingency Order:** Imposes certain limitations beyond the quantity and delivery month. Contingency orders may specify limits in price or time, or both.

**Discretionary Order:** Specifies quantity and option but does not specify prices. To be filled if and when the broker chooses.

**Straight Cancel Order:** Cancels the order in the pit or enters a new order once the former order has been canceled by the pit broker.

**One Cancels Other:** States two different execution possibilities with the broker's understanding that if one side of the OCO is executed, the other is automatically cancelled.

**Open Order:** Customer order that will continue to be placed in the pit until it is executed or canceled by the customer. Open orders can exist for long periods of time.

**Spread Orders:** Simultaneous purchase and sale of one commodity of different options.

**Stop Close Only:** Similar to a stop order except that it may be executed in the closing range only if it is above the buy stop price and below the sell stop price.

### *Spread Combinations*

**Butterfly:** Two equal and opposite spread positions in the same commodity that share one common contract month. For example, a position of buying 1 March 1986 US treasury bond, selling 2 June 1986 US treasury bonds, and buying 1 September 1986 US treasury bond is a butterfly.

**Condor:** Two equal and opposite spreads in the same commodity that do not share any contract months. For example, a position of buying 1 March 1986 US treasury bond, selling 1 June 1986 US treasury bond, selling 1 September US treasury bond, and buying 1 December US treasury bond is a condor.

**Tandem:** Two equal and opposite spread positions in related commodities that have exactly the same contract months. For example, buying 1 March 1986 GNMA, selling 1 June 1986 GNMA, selling 1 March US treasury bond, and buying 1 June 1986 US treasury bond is a tandem.

# Glossary

**Account Executive:** Employee of a firm who provides up-to-the-second market analysis on the trading floor to the firm's institutional clients.

**Arbitrage:** The buying (or selling) of one commodity and the simultaneous selling (or buying) of the same or similar commodity in a different market in an effort to profit from price discrepancies between the two related markets.

**Arbitration:** The process through which outtrades are resolved, usually by a board of exchange members.

**Brokerage House:** Firms that transact commodity business on the exchange floor on behalf of customers who may be either commercial users of the commodity markets or private investors.

**Clearing Corporation:** Serves as a giant link at an exchange by taking the opposite side of every trade made. Acts as an insurance agent by transferring the risk of fulfillment of the trades from individual brokerage houses to the clearing corporation, whose finances are backed by the combined forces of all its member firms.

**Commercial Hedgers:** Any commercial enterprise that uses the futures markets for hedging purposes. (see hedging)

**Contract:** A term used to stipulate the particular size of any commodity traded on an exchange. Used most commonly in a phrase such as, "I bought 5 corn contracts." One corn contract consists of 5,000 bushels. or "I sold 1 swiss franc contract." One swiss franc contract consists of 125,000 swiss francs.

**Deck:** The term used to describe the group of orders of any particular broker.

**Exchange:** The place where commodities are traded. A list of all the U.S. exchanges appears on pages 11 and 12.

**Fill:** An order that has been executed.

**Hedging:** A relatively complicated trading strategy used by banks and other large money managers to guard against adverse price movements. Usually involves the sale of futures contracts in anticipation of future sales of cash commodities as a protection against possible price declines, or the purchase of futures contracts in anticipation of future purchases of cash commodities as a protection against the possibility of increasing costs.

**Local:** A term used to describe an independent floor trader. A local may be a speculator, a scalper, or a spreader, but all locals trade for themselves from the floor.

**Margin:** A specific amount of good-faith money used to cover the risks inherent in any trade.

**Margin Clerk:** Person who insures a firms financial security by screening applicants, monitoring position of accounts, and recommending preventive measures.

**Outtrade:** Trade that does not have an equal and opposite side.

**Outtrade Clerk:** Person who works part-time in the morning and is responsible for alerting a firm's customers of their out trades.

**Quotation Screen:** A television-like screen that shows the changing commodity prices.

**Quotations Clerk:** Person who sits by the side of the trading pit and is responsible for punching up the changing prices to the quotations board and the ticker-tape.

**Runner:** The person who carrys customers orders to and from the order desk and broker pit.

**S & P:** Standard and Poor's 500 is a popular stock index which tracks the price movements of a group of 500 stocks. The Chicago Mercantile Exchange trades a S & P futures index.

**Scalping:** A short-term trading strategy that tries to take advantage of small, incremental price changes. In contrast to speculating, scalping doesn't involve anticipating long-term market movement, only split-second changes.

**Speculation:** A text book definition might be a trading strategy that tries to anticipate commodity price changes by either buying in anticipation of a price increase or selling in anticipation of a price decrease. A simpler definition is the act of betting whether a commodity will go up or down by either buying or selling it.

**Spreading:** The simultaneous buying (or selling) of one commodity and the selling (or buying) of another in the expectation of a changing price relationship between the two so that an offsetting purchase will yield a profit.

**Tandem and Butterfly:** These are in the list of orders (see appendix).

**Tick:** 1/32 of a point in the treasury bond contract at the CBOT.

**Ticker-Tape:** Usually an electronic board that shows the changing commodity prices.

**Time and Sales:** The exchange body that keeps the official record of all trades.

**Time Stamps:** A market fraud protection devise which is required by law and prints the date and time of an order to the nearest second.

**Trading Cards:** Basic cards on which brokers and locals record their trades.

**Trade Checker:** Person who works part-time after the close of the market and insures that each trade is properly recorded, including the price, quantity, and brokerage house.

**Trading Edge:** A term used by floor traders to describe buying at the bid and selling at the offer. "Bid" and "offer" refer, respectively, to the buy price and the sell price of a commodity at a particular instant in the market.

# Index